AF488865

Kuki Worship Service: Towards Community Transformation

Kuki Worship Service: Towards Community Transformation

Nkthang Haokip

2012

Kuki Worship Service: Towards Community Transformation- Published by the Rev. Dr. Ashish Amos of the Indian Society for Promoting Christian Knowledge (ISPCK), Post Box 1585, 1654, Madarsa Road, Kashmere Gate, Delhi-110006 .

© Author, 2012. *Christ for Gam le Nam*

All rights reserved. No part of this book may be reproduced or transmitted in any form or by any means, electronic, mechanical, photocopying, recording, or by any information storage and retrieval system, without the prior permission in writing from the publisher.

The views expressed in the book are those of the author and the publisher takes no responsibility for any of the statements.

ISBN: 978-81-8465-193-5

Laser typeset by

ISPCK, Post Box 1585, 1654, Madarsa Road, Kashmere Gate, Delhi-110006 • *Tel:* 23866323

e-mail: ashish@ispck.org.in • ella@ispck.org.in
website: www.ispck.org.in

Dedication

KUKI WORSHIP SERVICE
(K u k i t e   H o u k h a w m n a   N a t o h)

IN HONOUR OF
The First Baptised Man Among the Biate

Late Pu THIAICHONGNGOLA THIANGLAI
Saipum Village, NC Hills, Assam, 1890

The first Convert, Teacher and Ordained Pastor among the
Bawms

Late Pu Rev. KUALTHANG BAWITLUNG
Tlangpikhua Village, Bandarban Dist. CHT, Bangladesh

And

My Beloved Grandfather

Late Pu H.T. HOLNGAM
Maokot Church Founder, Ukhrul District, Manipur, 1937

Contents

ACKNOWLEDGEMENTS

God's *(Chung Pathien)* graceful guidance helped me do a theological course and undergo ministerial training. I performed these tasks in response to God's call.

I am grateful to KWS-Kolkata and all the valued members of KWS-London for their prayer and financial support during my study and to AIKWSCC for its plan and purpose. Also, I am thankful to Madam Amenla Aier, her husband Dr. Samuel Longkumer and Dr. K. P. Aleaz, Bishop's College, Kolkata, for their corrective concern. Thanks are due to Lhunkhosei Mate, Paulpaolen Haokip, Satkhokai Chongloi and Jangkholam Haokip for encouraging and supporting me during my research. I am also thankful to the leaders and members of KWS-Shillong, KWS-Happy Valley and KWS-Guwahati for their cooperation.

I remain grateful to the following persons for helping me with my theological studies and ministerial training: Rev. Dino L. Touthang and his wife Nu Dari Touthang, Rev. Paothang and his wife Nu Ruby Haokip, Mrs. Neihlamvaiphei Gerbaldi, Mr. Chonminlen Gangte, my sister Nenghoi Blackburn, Nu Tinnu and her husband Rev. Canon David Tongkhoyam and Rev. Dr. Letkhothang and his wife Dr. Nengboi Haokip.

My special thanks go to Pu Haojakhup Kipgen and his wife Pi Lamboi Kipgen, Rev. Biaksangliana Vaiphei and his wife V. Lalromingi, Mr. Khupkholal Doungel, Pa Tohkhopao Haokip and his wife Lamkimchan, Bro. Seiminlen (Jempu and Kimboi), Ms. Mary Chinkholhing, Mr. T. H. Robert, Mr. Lallenthang Lhouvum and Mr. Thangngalun Misao. I am also thankful to my brother Yampao and his wife Lhaikhoneng for supporting me in various ways.

Also, I am grateful to ISPCK for agreeing to publish this book.

FOREWORD

The diversity found Christianity in India makes it essential that micro-level studies are undertaken to describe the various facets of the Christian faith in a region or among a particular people. The Kuki *diaspora* are part of the great diversity in Indian Christianity. So, the forms that Church life and life of faith take in this community are an important field of study. The academic study that Mr. Nkthang Haokip has undertaken will certainly assist both ordinary Church members and theologians in gaining a deeper insight into the history and form of Church life among the Kuki *diaspora*. Based on primary sources, this book has facts about Kuki tribes, Kuki Christians and theological discussions considered from the indigenous Kuki perspective. Indeed, this book contributes a lot towards the development of Kuki theology.

I warmly recommend this book to all those who are interested in Christianity in India.

January 2012

Revd. Dr. Sunil M. Caleb,
Principal, Bishop's College,
Kolkata

INTRODUCTION

Kuki Worship Service: Towards Community Transformation

In this study, an attempt has been made to find out whether Kuki Worship Service (KWS) serves as one of the unifying and transformative factors among the Kukis in the midst of prevailing divisions.

Among the interconnected dialect-communities of the Kukis, church doctrinal or church organisational worship is carried out in different ways. The communities are divided in the name of doctrine, church organisation, denominational association and system of worship. A system of *Houbung*[1] prevails among the people.

Socially, ancestral names are misused in the name of *phung le chang*.[2] The prevailing close circle of marriage forms the basis for close-minded relationships leading to a narrow outlook. This practice usually acts as a catalyst for social evil.

---

[1] Literally Houbung (*Hou=worship, bung=group*) Houbung means to worship in group.

[2] *Phung* means tree (family tree) and *chang* means section or branch.

However, "Diaspora Kukis"[3] come together in the service of Christ as a community in *"Pathien Oi."*[4] KWS functions as one of the uniting factors in different cities. In this study, an attempt has been made to find out whether KWS acts as a tool for unification and transformation in the Kuki community as a whole. Also, this study focuses on KWS in certain established cities with a special focus on eastern India.

The first chapter of the book introduces the reader to the Kuki people. It also looks at their settlement, custom, culture, tradition, folk tales and administration of polity.

The second chapter focuses on the history of Kuki worship service with a special reference to formation and growth of KWS units in different regions and cities of India. It also looks at KWS in and outside India and the formation and functions of All India Kuki Worship Service Coordinating Committee (AIKWSCC).

The third chapter reviews the role played by KWS in unifying and transforming the Kuki people.

The fourth chapter gives a theological response to KWS and theology of Kuki humanity for unification and transformation of people. It also looks at the Khankho way of life.

---

[3] The Kuki people who live abroad to pursue education, employment, business and the like.

[4] Literally Pathien (literally, *Pa*=Father and *thien*=Holy) Holy-father, God. Traditionally *Oi* means "to accept with faithful trust." Originally and traditionally, *Pathien*/Pathian/Pasian is known by the Chin-Kuki-Mizo People as benevolent God, most high and powerful in Spirit to sustain or recreate. *Pathien Oi* refers to "People of Faith" who "Trust God's Word" of the Bible called *Pathien thu awih* and adhere to the Gospel of Christ Jesus. It means life is with *Pathien* (God) and *Pathien* lives within the human person in spirit. Early believers' adherence to the Gospel of Jesus Christ led the believers to become *Pathien Oi*, messianic people of faith in Christ.

ABBREVIATIONS

AIKWSCC	All India Kuki Worship Service Coordinating Committee
CE	Common Era
ECCI	Evangelical Congregational Church of India
ECFI	Eimi Christian Fellowship Chennai
FMPB	Friend Missionary Prayer Band
ICCC	Indian Campus Crusade for Christ
KWS	Kuki Worship Service
KCLF	Kuki Christian Leaders Fellowship
KSO	Kuki Students' Organisation
KSDF	Kuki Students Democratic Front
KNO	Kuki National Organisation
KUMHUR	Kuki Movement for Human Rights
NEHU	North Eastern Hill University
SHG	Self Help Group
SoO	Suspension of Operation
TTS	Trulock Theological Seminary

UPF   United People Front

OTC   Oriental Theological College

CHAPTER ONE

Understanding Indigenous Kuki Tribes

INTRODUCTION

The Bible is a book of the word of God and a human document. It is the outcome of the inspirational work of the Spirit of the Creatorcarried out through humans. A theological researcher needs to find out whether it is necessary to trace the origin of human community in the light of the Creation narrative. The origin and growth of Kuki tribes should be traced in the light of not only the creation narrative, but also the oral tradition of the Kukis, anthropological findings and the available historical evidence.

Indigenous Kuki Tribes

'Kuki'[1] is a generic term used to refer to the Kuki people (clans and tribes).[2] Kuki (Cuci) means "mountainous people" or "highlander"[3] The Kuki people are indigenous groups of hill

---

[1] *Cooci, Kookie, Cuci* and *Kukie* are the different spellings of "Kuki" as used by western writers in English.

[2] Tarun Goswami, *Kuki Life and Lore* (Haflong: NC Hills District Council, Assam 1985), 1.

[3] William Shaw, *Notes on the Thadou-Kukis* (Guwahati: Maranatha Printing Press, 1929), 10.

people who settled in the Independent Hill Country.[4] A study of the anthropology and culture of the *Leisanpa* reveals the origins and identity of the Kuki people as based on *Themthu-Lapi*.[5] The origin of the Kuki people is shrouded in myths and

---

[4] *The Kuki People and their Country* (Washington DC: The Publicity Wing Kuki Movement for Human Rights, 2005) 2-3. Reference to R.C. Majundar & N Bhattacharya. *History of India*. (1930, pp. 6-7), 5th revised edition.

[5] Khuplam Milui Lenthang, *Reports of Seminar on Manmasi Identity* (Imphal: LB Printer, 2009), 5-6. (*Themthu-Lapi* is a Kuki primal religious incantation and chanting verse of oral tradition). His report stated that the Chin-Kuki-Mizo originated as *LEISANPA*; literally means "red-soil man", (the first human on earth; Gen. 2:7). A rough translation of *themthu* is as follows: *He, he, he yah! The maker of red-soil man, who came from above, taking care of him. The descendents of the red-soil man inhabited the entire earth. Selah!* The chant is repeated two to three times and the priest sets free the second rooster in the wilderness as an offering to *Noijinmaangpa* (Lord of the Subterranean). The same ritual is practiced by the children of Mamasi (Lev 16: 8-10). The priest then collects the unbroken bones of the sacrificial rooster, and starting from his right side, proceeds towards the paddy field without looking back, followed by the helpers. On reaching the hut of the field, the priest places unbroken bones in the small bamboo basket called *doibom*, which is normally hung on a pole within the courtyard, and then the priest begins another chant (translation of the *themthu*): *He he he yah, I lay unbroken bones of white rooster in the Doibom (themthulhunbom) for sound mind, sound health, good fortune, abundance of food grains and abundant wealth and livestock.* After supplication for blessing and good fortune for the children of Manmasi, the priest places the broken bone in the *doibom (themthulhunbom)*; the ritual concludes in a convivial atmosphere with members of team taking turns to imbibe through a bamboo straw traditional rice wine brewed in an earthen jar. Failure to perform the ritual of *Leisanpa* is believed to incur the wrath of God upon the children of Manmasi, which is manifested in the form of epidemics, diseases and scarcity of food. (*Themthulhunbom* means a container of all the words, that is, *Doibom*, the powerful spiritual words of box, locally constructed according to the advice of the *thempu*, used by the primal Kuki priest). However, there are several historians and writers who have draw the conclusion that the Kuki-Chin people originated in Mongolia and belonged to the Mongolian race. This inference has

mythologies. According to a traditional account, Kukis came out of the bowels of the earth or a subterranean place called *Chinlung* or *Sinlung* or *Khul*.[6] It may be noted that the Aryans who drove the Dravidians towards the south arrived in the Indian sub-continent around 1500 BCE.[7] Concerning the origin of Kuki, E. B. Elly, a British official, wrote, in 1893, that the term "Kuki", meaning "hill people", originated in Sylhet in former East Bengal.[8] The Kuki group in Chittagong Hill Tracts are called *Tlangmi*.[9] In the *Pooyas*, the traditional records of the Meitei people of Manipur, dated Kuki at 33 CE. The two Kuki chiefs, Kuki Ahongba and Kuki Achouba, were allies to Nongba Lairen Pakhangba, the first historically recorded king of the Meithis (Meiteis).[10] In the second century (CE 90–168), Claudius Ptolemy, the geographer, identified the Kukis with Tiladai, who are associated with Tilabharas, and placed them "to the north of Maiandros, that is about the Garo Hills and Silhet." In Rajmala or Annals of Tripura, Shiva is quoted to have fallen in love with a Kuki damsel around 1512 CE.[11]

---

generally been accepted because those researches do not go beyond Mongolia and no researcher has focused on *Themthu-Lapi*. Noted scientists and anthropologists state that the theory that human beings descended from the monkeys contradicts the account of the origin of man given in the Bible.

[6] T. S. Gangte, *op.cit.*, *p.19*

[7] *The Kuki People and their Country* (Washington DC: The Publicity Wing Kuki Movement for Human Rights, 2005), 2-3. Reference to R.C. Majumdar & N Bhattacharya. *History of India.* (1930, p6-7), 5th revised edition.

[8] E. B. Elly, *Military Report on the Chin-Lushai Country*, (Calcutta: KLM Pvt. Ltd, 1978), 1.

[9] Local Kuki dialect terms *Tlangmi/Thinglhaangmi* or *Singtaangmi* means mountainuos or hill forest people or highlander in English.

[10] N. P. Rakung, *Reader in The Telegraph*, 17 January 1994, Letter to the Editor, Imphal, Manipur.

[11] According to *Cheitharol Kumaba, Royal Chronicles of the Meitei Kings*, in the year 186, Sakabda (AD 264) Meidungu Taothingmang, a Kuki became king.

Another generic term that refers to the Kukis in the twentieth century is "Mizo." Kuki and Mizo comprise numerous agnate clans with shared cultural roots.[12] The other nomenclatures of latterly origin, such as Mizo, Zomi and Bawm, have emerged to identify the same people. Their interconnected dialects are classified linguistically under the Tibeto-Burman group of languages.[13] The Kukis emphasise the concept of nationalism in relation to unification under a common identity. In the context of India, which is a nation-state, the Kukis can only be a group of tribes or indigenous tribes, not national identity. Kuki is only a conglomerate name of the Indigenous People of Tribes (IPT). So, the Kukis are categorised under the Scheduled Tribe list as "Any Kuki Tribes."[14]

---

[12] Seilen Haokip, *Rhetoric of Kuki Nationalism, A Treatise* (New Delhi: Lustra Print, 2010), 15.

[13] Horatio Bickerstaffe Rowney, *The Wild Tribes of India* (Delhi: Low Price Publication, 1982), 179-189.

[14] "Any Kuki tribes", Register No. DL.33004/2003 *The Gazette of India Extraordinary*, Part II, Section I, Published by Authority New Delhi, Wednesday Jan 8, 2003, Ministry of Law and Justice (Legislative Department), Subject Schedule Caste and Schedule Tribe orders (Amendment Act, 2002) No. 10 of 2003 (J) in part x- Manipur , p6. "Any Kuki Tribes" A to Z includes: *Aimol, Anal, Baite, Biete, Belalhut, Changsan, Chhalya , Chiru, Chongloi, Chothe, Doungel, Fua, Gangte, Guite, Gamalhou, Hanneng, Hajango, Hangshing, Hmar, Haokip or Haupit, Haolai, Hengna, Hongsungh, Hrangkhwal or Rangkhol, Jangtei, Jongbe, Khawchung, Khawathlang or Khothalong, Khelma, Kholhou, Kipgen, Kharam, Koireng, Kolhen, Khoreng, Khephong, Kuntei, Kuki, Kom, Khyang Lakher, Laifang, Lentei, Lamkang, Lenthang (Telien), Lepcha, Lhanghal, Lhangum, Lhouvum, Lhungdim, Lunkim, Lhoujem , Lhouvum, Lupheng, Maring, Mate, Mizel , Milhem, Misao, Monshang, Muyon, Mro, Paite, Paitu, Purum, Riang, Rangchan, Sarihem or Sairhem, Seinam or Selnam, Simte, Singsit, Sitlhou, Singson, Sukte, Thado/Thadou, Thangluya, Thangngeu, Tarao, Touthang, Urbuh or Uibuh, Vaiphei, Zou.*

Settlement of the Kukis

It has been historically proved that the area within the latitude lines 20°5 "N to 25° 5" N and longitude lines 90°3 "E to 95°4" E[15] is the native land of the Kukis. Originally, "Kuki", is the name given to the tribes inhabiting both sides of the mountains dividing Assam and Bengal from Burma, South of the Namtaleik river."[16] "Kuki" is an ethnic group of people living in Burma, Nagaland, Assam, Tripura, Mizoram and Manipur of North-East India."[17] Stevenson's reference to "Kuki" in relation to Ptolemy's Geography also bears critical significance to its period existence.[18] According to *Encyclopædia Britannica*, Captain Dun has written that "the whole of wild tribes who dwell in the mountain districts contained between Bengal, Burma, Cachar, Manipur and Arakan have conceived the designation Kuki, all these tribes have so many common grounds of affinity that the classification seemed to have been, however accident, correct."[19]

Land is of paramount importance to the Kukis. In fact, their livelihood depends on it. *Lal* or *Haosa* is the landlord in which the big brother *Toupa/mi'upa* is the head, and the family depends upon his administration. God has given enough space on earth

---

[15] Closed landmark area called the Home of the Kuki Tribes by *George Abraham Grierson (1851-1941)*, marked out by *Lhunkhosei Mate* and the author with reference to the Reader's Digest, *Great World Atlast*. London.

[16] *Encyclopaedia Britannica* Vol-13. (1962), 511

[17] See also *http://en.wikipedia.org/wiki/Kuki* (*June 24*, 2010. 2:41 PM)

[18] Stevenson, EL (ed) (1932), Claudius Ptolemy: *The Geography*, (2nd century), translated and edited by Edward Luther Stevenson, Dover edition, first published in 1991 (p.xiii), an unabridged republication of the work originally published by The New York Public Library, N.Y., 1932, Dover Publications, Inc. New York

[19] E. W. Dun, *Gazetteer of Manipur*, (Delhi: Vivek Publication Company, 1981), 32.

to the Kukis to lead fulfilling lives. But some of the more civilised nations came to the "Land of Kukis", and the land and people came under alien rule.[20]

The British were the first to invade the Kuki Country — also known as Independent Hill Country or Land of Freedom, *Zale'n Gam*, the Kuki land of freedom. *Zale'n Gam* refers to the contiguous ancestral lands situated in present-day North-East India, Northwest Burma and the Chittagong Hill Tracts in Bangladesh. The Kukis are the indigenous tribes of *Zale'n Gam*.[21]

> The Kuki Inpi (Kuki Government) had defended the entire country for its indigenous inhabitants since 1761 CE. The last and greatest battle was fought between the years 1917 and 1919 which many scholars named 'The Kuki Rebellion' or 'The Kuki Rising' or 'The Kuki War of Independence' etc. Kuki Chiefs were asked to surrender under the British colonial rule, which was refused because they chose imprisonment in order to save their country by which act of bravery, this independent hill country remained under the chiefs as it was before. Before any political settlement has ever been done with the Kuki people, the British had left the land since they had granted political freedom to their colonized India in 1947 and Burma in 1948. The Kukis were evenly distributed without their consent and the Independent Hill Country did not merge into or join the Indian Union or Burma but remained as it is today.[22]

---

[20] Nehkholun Kipgen, *Why not Kukiland*, Ahsijolneng annual magazine (A publication of Kuki Students' Organization 2007), 17.

[21] P.S. Haokip, *Zale'n Gam The Kuki Nation* (KNO Publication, 2008), 1. The Kuki term, *Zale'n Gam* means the "Land of Freedom" in English. *Zale'n Gam* is the Kuki Land of Freedom where the traditional *Kuki Inpi* existed.

[22] *The plight of the indigenous Kuki people, unraveling the story of deception, suppression and marginalization in the trio border areas of India, Myanmar and Bangladesh* (Imphal: Kuki Movements for Human Rights, 2009), 1.

George Abraham Grierson (1851-1941) describes the Kuki Country in the Linguistic Survey of India:

> The territory inhabited by the Kuki tribes extends from the Naga Hills in the north down into the Sandoway District of Burma in the south; from Myittha River in the east, almost to the Bay of Bengal in the west. It is almost entirely filled up by hills and mountain ridges, separated by deep valleys.
>
> A great chain of mountains suddenly rises from the plains of Eastern Bengal, about 220 miles north of Calcutta, and stretches eastward in a broadening mass of spurs and ridges, called successively the Garo, Khasia, and Naga Hills. The elevation of the highest point increases towards the east, from about 3,000 feet in the Garo Hills to 8,000 and 9,000 in the region of Manipur.
>
> This chain merges, in the east, into the spurs, which the Himalayas shoot out from the north of Assam towards the south. From here, a great mass of mountain ridges starts southwards, enclosing the alluvial valley of Manipur, and thence spreads out westwards to the south of Sylhet. It then runs almost due north and south, with cross-ridges of smaller elevation, through the districts known as the Chin Hills, the Lushai Hills, Hill Tipperah, and the Chittagong Hill Tracts. Farther south the mountainous region continues, through the Arakan Hill tracts, and the Arakan Yoma, until it finally sinks into the sea at Cape Negrais, the total length of the range being some seven hundred miles.
>
> The greatest elevation is found to the north of Manipur. Thence it gradually diminishes towards the south. Where the ridge enters the north of Arakan it again rises, with summit upwards of 8,000 feet high, and here a mass of spurs is thrown off in all directions. Towards the south the western offshoots diminish in length, leaving a track of alluvial land between them and the sea, while in the north the eastern offshoots of the Arakan Yoma run down to the banks of the Irawaddy.
>
> This vast mountainous region, from the Jaintia and Naga Hills in the north, is the home of the Kuki tribes. We find them, besides, in the valley of Manipur, and, in small settlements, in the Cachar Plains and Sylhet.[23]

---

[23] G. A. Grierson, *Linguistic Survey of India,* Vol. III. (Calcutta: Asiatic Society), Part 3.

It has yet to dawn upon the minds of many of our leaders that the ideology of the people and ethnicity are more important than nomenclature. Besides the inclusive "Any Kuki Tribes" Suspension of Operations (SoO) is also an important factor in the enhancement of Kuki unity. The purpose of SoO is to hold tripartite dialogue for a viable political settlement for the Kuki people within the Constitution of India.[24]

Traditional Kuki Polity

Political autonomy is the birthright of the Kukis. It was sealed within the Kuki chiefdom called *Haosatna Gam* or *Kuki-Lalna Gam* is the "Kukiland of freedom." The traditional Kuki system of polity came into being when a group of clans started living together in villages.

The traditional Kuki polity can be classified into three levels:

- The family level
- The village level
- The national level

Family Level

Traditionally, in the culture of the Kuki patriarch society, man takes woman and woman accepts to become a family with her man and his kin's circle family. Husband and wife become parents and a new household is established as "Family

---

[24] Haokip, *Rhetoric of Kuki nationalism...*, 40. States that: *Suspension of Operation* signed on 10 August 2005 between Indian Army and KNO, followed by another SoO on 22 August 2008 signed among Government of India, KNO and the state Government of Manipur. UPF's political objective is identical to KNO's in terms of the people and land. On the one hand, pre-occupation with an alternative to the terminology Kuki, and on the other hand, considerations of regional issues seems to be an obstacle in the two umbrella organisations shaking hands to forge unity, as cited by Dr. Seilen.

Administration" called *Insung Kivaipoh*.[25] Family administration consists of the following responsible persons; these people are traditionally appointed according to the custom of the Kukis:

- A married man is appointed as the spokesman. Traditionally, he is known to preserve the title called *Be* or *Bepa*. Two or more persons can be appointed with the customary titles *Bebul* (head) and *Becha* (supplementary).

- The term *Tute* is a customary term that refers to the relationship that a woman who has procured a husband has with the household. The eldest daughter's household is customarily called *Tubul* (head), and *Tucha* is the title given to the younger daughters' household, if it exists.

- The term *Sunggao*, another traditional title, refers to a mother's brother or son. Traditionally, the *sunggao* people can claim the *long-man* (price of dead body) of mother.

- The term *Nulam* refers to the relationship among the households who have procured wives from the same family. All the men who take wives from one household are known as *nulam*.

The patriarchal custom of Kuki paterfamilias relationship is known as *U-pa–Naopa*.[26] It is a system of male-kin circle headed by the eldest man called *U-pa*, which means *Big Brother* (known as *Toupa*). Administration is established with the existing house

---

[25] Traditionally, the eldest married son followed up the reign of his father but the younger son(s) had to create and establish family administration according to the custom through the advice or help of his father or elders.

[26] *U-pa* means "elder" and *naopa* means "younger."

of the genealogically known eldest "Head", which is known as *Sating Lhunna*.[27] The traditionally known authority of the "House of Eldest" is called *U-pa Inpi*. This authority is not just about having power. It entails responsibility and ethical obligation according to custom and culture. The various levels of *U-pa Inpi* involve taking care of family, sub-clans, clan and eventually the whole group of a tribe confederation. The authority of the House of *U-pa* is traditionally honoured as a decision-making body responsible for settling clanmen's family issues. There is one *U-pa* for one section of Kuki clans; for example, Chengjapao Doungel, Chief of Aisan village, served a long imprisonment under the British regime after the Anglo-Kuki war (1917-1919).[28]

Village Level

The village "chiefdom", which is called the *Haosa-gam* territory of a chief *(Haosa)* and his *Haosatna*, means "chieftainship." It was the basic begetter of sovereign Kuki polity before the arrival of the British in India. This traditional polity was complemented by governing bodies such as:

- *Semang* (person in charge of home affairs)
- *Pachong* (person responsible for defence and external affairs)
- *Lhaangsam* (spokesperson of public relations and broadcasting)
- *Lawm-Upa* (person in charge of youth, economic and cultural affairs)

---

[27] *Sating lhunna:* The backbone of animal given to the eldest or genealogically known head of the family entitled him as *Mi'upa* (being the backbone of a clan family).

[28] Chongloi, *op.cit., pp.132-133*

- *Thiempu* (the priest)
- *Toullai-Pao* (the law and order enforcement person)[29]

Kuki Nampi Level

At the national (nampi) level, governance is known as *Kuki Inpi* (the Kuki government). The pattern is replicated at the *Lhaang* (the district) level and *Gamkai* (the state) level. Integral to Kuki polity is *Inpi*, the apex body, of which each village chief is a member. *Inpi* executes policies and programmes to tackle matters of high importance. The traditional *Kuki Inpi*, which remained latent for many years, was revived following the crises faced by the Kukis during the 1980s and 1990s.[30] The Kuki portfolios and power in chiefdom were traditionally dignified with the spirit of *tawmngaihna*[31] in service and dedication. The Kuki way of life and polity are essentially socialistic in nature.

Kuki Folk Tales

The Kukis' commonality finds its expression in Kuki folk tales. As in the past so also in the present, these tales act as a binding force among the Kukis. Legendary tales like *Chemtatpa* or *Temtatpu, Khalvompu, Changkhatpu and Ahsijolneng, Khalvompu and Lenchonghoi* or *Lengtonghoih* are still very popular in the Kuki region. The diversity of Kuki culture is seen in tales like *Chapinthei le Mailangkoh, Lhangeineng* and so on. The folklore of the Kukis abounds with the heroic adventures of *Galngam le Hangsai, Chemtatpa, Lengbante, Jamdil, Sangah le Ahpi*, etc. Poignant romantic tales such as *Khupting le Ngambom, Jonlhing*

---

[29] See also *http://www.kukination.net/government.php*

[30] See also *http://www.kukination.net/history.php*

[31] *Tawmngaihna* is a traditional custom of self-sacrificial service in response to the situation demand in time of need.

le Nanglhun, Changkhatpu le Ahshijolneng and *Khalvompu le Lenchonghoi* have played a vital role in binding the Kukis together.[32]

Kuki Custom, Culture and Tradition

Festivals, special rites and deaths give us a glimpse into the folklore of the Kukis.

Chhangvai

Chhangvai is a traditional way of hunting animals in this region. A group of men or women hunts animals in the range of *Sadel-lhaang*[33] jungle hill forest. They set off with musical instruments like *khong/khuang* (local drum), *selki* (animal horn) and *pengkul* (local trumpet) and tools like *thaangkuol* (robes of trap), *chempong* (daos), *chemjam* (sword), *thalpi* (arrow), *meithal* (gun), etc. They normally chase the animal while playing the musical instruments. The animal is slowly surrounded on three sides and is either caught or killed on the fourth side.

Sa-ai *and* Chaang-ai

Sa-ai[34] is a victorious cheer of courage performed by the village folk. The subjugator of the animal and his folk celebrate the capture of the animal with *haanla*—the Song of Courage.[35] Traditionally, a man who can hunt strong animals such as tigers,

---

[32] PS Haokip *op., cit, 84.*

[33] *Sadel-lhaang* (*sa* means animal, *del* means to hunt and *lhaang* means range of hills/mountain) refers to the range of hills/mountains where animals used to be hunted.

[34] The word *sa* means animal and *ai* means applause or cheer (applausive cheers due to the subjugation of an animal).

[35] *Haanla* the"traditional ballad of courage" began with "Kathange! Kathange!" which means "renowned is my name", and the ballad ends with "li. li. li. li. li, li..." Then folk would reply with humming cheers "Ho, ho, ho, ho, ho, ho..."

leopards, bears and elephants is greatly honoured in the area. *Chaang-Ai*[36] celebrates the role played by the womenfolk in the production of rice. It is a thanksgiving festival: The women are thanked for their fruitful labour.[37] Traditionally, providing meat for the family and for the occasional feasting of villagers was regarded as the duty of a man and procuring sufficient grain was regarded as the duty of a woman in the family.[38] There is a traditional saying that a person who performs the *Sa-ai* well and participates fully in *Chaang-ai* celebration gains peaceful transition to a life in paradise.

Lawm

Lawm[39], which literally means "team work" or "corporate labour", is a traditional Kuki organisation meant for socio-economic stability. The main objectives of *Lawm* are:

- To develop a sense of responsibility among the youth in the collective spirit of *tawmngaihna* social service

- To bring about economic development in the village by corporate work in the fields on a rotational basis

- To serve as a training centre for youths, where they could learn about the various methods of cultivation and develop the habit of charity so that they do not find it difficult to help the needy, the destitute and the widows in the village.

---

[36] The word *chaang* means paddy and *ai* refers to victory of the soul of paddy (Festival of the abundance of rice production).

[37] See also *http://www.kukination.net/culture.php*

[38] Hemkhochon Chongloi, *Indoi. A study of primal Kuki religious symbolism in the hermeneutical framework of Mircea Eliade* (Delhi: ISPCK, 2008). 141.

[39] *Lawm* refers to traditionally known *organisation*, while some writers use it to mean *lom* , which means "a bunch."

A mature man or woman of every household in the region is a member of *Lawm*. To work in the field of every member in rotation regardless of the capability of each individual member of *Lawm* is their important service. The organisation consists of various office bearers with different duties or assignments. The main functionary leader of *Lawm* is *Lawm-Upa* (elder of the *Lawm*). His duty is to maintain discipline among the members. *Lawm-Lhaangsam* or *Tollaipao* (the spokesperson) is the next in hierarchy. This spokesperson uses his *Taithing Tenggol* (walking stick) to maintain discipline among the members from morning till dusk. *Lawm-Pengkul Mut* (the trumpeter) blows his trumpet while ordering routine of daily activities. *Lawm-Upanu* (woman-leader) keeps strong vigilance over discipline among women and looks after *Lawm-Becha/ Tucha* (supervisors) and *Lawm-Twikhai* (water supply group) as well. The younger members of *Lawm* are normally responsible for supplying water.[40] This organisation also functions as an agent for reforming personal character by fostering the art and spirit of *tawmngaina* among the members.

Shom

Shom[41] is an active bachelors' dormitory that is normally set up in a household. This is where the young people learn about their role in society and the value of other essential responsibilities in political, military and economic spheres. *Shom-Upa* (the leader of *shom*) is responsible for managing *shom*. The village chief is the *de facto* authority of *shom* by virtue of his position, but he does not interfere in its day-to-day administration. Each *shom* had two types of members, namely senior and junior. *Shom* is also like a family and its members

---

[40] PS Haokip *op.cit, 78-79. See also http://www.kukination.net/culture.php*

[41] *Shom* refers to traditionally known *bachelor dormitory*. Some writers use it to mean *som,* which means counting number *ten.*

do household chores, such as repairing baskets, preparing cane splits to make strings called *naang* and collecting building materials from the forest. A *shomnu* (a young woman at *Shom*) knows her duties well. These duties consist of activities like mending young men's clothes, putting sleeping places in order, providing night blankets (woven at home), offering tobacco leaves and combing their hair.[42] *Shom* also functions as an education centre, where people acquire social virtues, develop discipline and undergo moral and psychological training. It also functions as a defence force and standing army. Despite intimate relationships and close association among unmarried men and women at *Shom*, promiscuousness and cases of unmarried pregnancy have not been reported till date.

Kuki Community Festivals

Kut is a traditional community festival of thanksgiving dedicated to *Chung Pathien*, the benevolent and supreme God. Given below are the names of the festivals in which the word *Kut* figures:

- The harvest of a special kind of local grain locally called *Mim* is celebrated as *Mim Kut*.

- *Chaang Kut* is a *kut* of rice harvest festival.

- The general festival of harvest is called *Pawl Kut*.

- *Chavang Kut* is an autumnal harvest festival of thanksgiving.

- Chapphou/Chapchar Kut.[43]

---

[42] Kuki boys and men traditionally sported long hair and were known as *tuhbemsom*

[43] *Chapphou* or *Chapchar* means preparation for jhum or swidden cultivation, which involves clearing of the land by the slash-and-burn method, celebrated as community festival *Chapphou/Chapchar Kut*.

The other community festivals are:

- *Lawm Sel Neh* is celebrated by young people when the seasonal work is over. They prefer to slaughter the local animal called *Sel* for the celebration.

- After the planting of grains and vegetables, comes the occasion for worship at which a white rooster is sacrificed without breaking any of its bones. This festival is known as rite of *Hun* or *Ahkangtha*.

- All the members of *Shom* and *Lawm* feast for their dedicated labours called *Shom Kivah* and *Lawm Kivah*. A convivial atmosphere prevails and people drink *zu* (local rice beer); feasting, dancing and singing are the integral part of the feasts. Traditional local games such as *kibot* (wrestling), *Teng-khaw/Song-se* (javelin- and pestle-throw), *Sel kal*[44] (high jump) and *Kangkaap* are a major highlight.[45] The nature of all the traditional festivals of the past reflects a state of peace, harmony and prosperity.

Lenkhawm

The two-syllable word *Len-khawm*[46] means "get-together." It is a social gathering that involves a lot of merrymaking: the air resounds with the beating of the traditional drum called *Khuong*

---

[44] Local big animal called *Mithun* or *bison* is made immobile by being fastened securely with poles to jump over

[45] PS Haokip. *op.cit, 81-82.*

[46] *Lenkhawm* (literally *len/laileng*) means to "step-out for meeting" and *khawm* means "together." Some writers use the spelling *lenkhom* , which refers to *lenkhawm*. It is practice of traditional *Shom* for the Kuki people who follow the teaching of *Jesu* because get-together in *lenkhawm* is said to have been formulated by the *Pathien-Oi* people after they left primal religious life.

or *khuang* and the songs of *Lathah Bu*, which are sung together.[47] The new songbook is called *Lathah Bu* because the songs that figure in it are not from English hymn books; they are very much indigenous and meant for the spirituality of the Kuki people.[48]*Shom Kivah* or *Lawm Kivah* is the originator of the modern *Lenkhawm*. Its importance grows when people console members of a bereaved family by singing songs of spiritual contentment. *Lenkhawm* has a unique meaning that has much in common with the teachings in the New Testament: Rejoice with those who rejoice; mourn with those who mourn in the days of sadness and happiness (Romans 12:15-16).

Religion

The word "religion" has no accurate equivalent in Kuki. The Kuki *homo religious* simply uses the term *Pu Hou-Pa Hou*, which may be translated as "that which the forebear worship."[49] However, the term *sakho*[50] comes nearest to expressing the meaning of the word "religion" as it points at the concept of

---

[47] *Lathah Bu* means "New Song Book." Paolen Haokip, *The impact of contemporary music on Christian worship with special reference to the Kuki Worship Service, Delhi*. Unpublished BD Thesis, Union Biblical Seminary, Pune, 2005), 29 states that *Lathah Bu* came into existence due to the efforts made by the Tamenglong Church through KCA and the responsibility to compile the songs was handed over to SL Jamkholal (Palal); to compile the song from Lushai *(Pathian Thu Awih group)* and others. Many people also used to called it *Palal Labu*, as cited by the statements of T. Lunkim and Rev. S. Prime Vaiphei.

[48] *Ibid.*, p.28-29

[49] Chongloi. *op., cit, 133.... Sakho* or *sakhua* is of the same meaning; it means religion of village people.

[50] *Sakho/Sakhua* is a rite of institution performed with a strong belief in supernatural power or divine power that can control human destiny as cited by Rev. Puia. *Sakho is Religion* as cited by Dr. T. Lunkim , "Religion and Politics" Guwahati , *Khanglai 2008 cum KWS-G Decade Celebration, Souvenir* (October, 2008), 62.

believing in the benevolent nature of God, *Chung Pathien*[51] (above/heavenly father)—the protector and sustainer of human life. The eternal nature of the Supreme Being is addressed as *Pathien* (Holy Father) or *Chung Pathien* (Holy Father of above).[52] The original term *Pathien* (Holy Father), which refers to God, has been drawn from ancient terminology.

The word *Pathien* (God) consists of two words: *Pa* (It literally means "father" and denotes the origin of all beings or a human person with respect and veneration) and *thien* refers to "sacredness", "holiness", "purity."[53] *Pathien* does not mean earthly human father who lives and reigns on earth with imperfections. This is indicated by the word *thien;* its derivative *thieng* (when suffixed with letter 'g') qualifies as "clean", "ideal", "sacred", "holy", "pure", etc. *Khankho*[54] gives a lot of importance to doing the will of *Pathien* because it is all about love and concern for others.[55] *Khankho* reflects the moral and ethical value of community life.

Kuki Primal Practise of Appeasement

The primal Kukis believed in the power of malevolent ghosts and benevolent spirits. It was generally believed that displeasing malevolent ghosts led to epidemics, diseases,

---

[51] *Pathien, Pasian* and *Pathian* are the same meaning and concept of the "Zo" conglomerate group of people.

[52] Chongloi. *op.cit,* 143.

[53] Paolen Haokip, "Karl Barth understanding of 'the word of God' and its relevance for Kuki understanding of Pathienthu (word of God) today." Unpublished Thesis: Senate of Serampore, NIIPGTS, Serampur, 2009), 41

[54] *Khankho* (literally, *khan* means "growth" and *kho* means "village"). Jangkholam Haokip, "Impact of Christianity" Guwahati , *Khanglai 2008 cum KWS-G Decade Celebration, Souvenir* (October, 2008), 61.

[55] Chongloi. *op.cit,* 130 and 134.

sicknesses and deaths. Primal priests, who were known as *thempu*, performed rites, which included sacrifice of domestic fowls and animals and chants of the words of *doi* (called *doithu*),[56] to appease evil spirits.[57] Some of the possessors of the malevolent ghost and places of malevolency are:

- The earthly malevolent ghost of death called *Thilha*, forest evil sprite called *gamhoise*, village evil sprite called *inmunse* and other evil entities.

- The *Lhangnel*,[58] which referred to a handsome entity with an aureole. It can transform itself into animals such as serpents, pythons, small snakes, wild cocks and elks. It is regarded as Lucifer, for it reigns in the lower world and is called *Noimaangpa* (lord of the underworld).[59]

- The source of water fountain in the jungle, which is called *siphung* or *sibo/nabo*; the owner of the water fountain is called *tuinahpa*.

- *Tuitopa* is the owner of the end of water fountain, where water flows away; it is the lower region where *Lhangnel* (Lucifer) reigns.[60]

---

[56] There are two types of *Doithu*: Words of incantation *indoi thu* or *themthu* are of life's supportive and nurturing *doi* and almost all *doithu* are life-giving and protecting words of power. However, the other types of *doi* that referred to the witchcraft words of witchery were also used by primal people against their enemy.

[57] T.S. Gangte, *op.cit.,161*.

[58] *Lhangnel:* literally *lhang* means "lower" and *nel* means "aureole" (a being of lower region that has an aureole).

[59] Chongloi. *op.cit, 139*.

[60] The primal people's understanding of *twinahpa* and *twitopa* was of personified evil-dwellers; however, *twinah* (water fountain) is the source of life's supporting place (humans cannot live without water) and *twito* (anus of water, where water flowed away, is accumulation of dirt and dung) is the end of life support; therefore, *twinah* and *twito* also mean the "beginning" and the "end" (called *alpha* and *omega* in Greek).

The abovementioned malevolent ghost needs to be pleased or appeased by the sacrifice of a purely domestic white fowl called *ahkang* or a purely black fowl called *ahvom*, or any other domestic animal, with chants of the words of *Doithu*. Healing is done through blood sacrifice and performance of the appropriate rite by the *thempu*.[61]

Kuki Worship Service

Kuki Worship Service (KWS) was first started in Shillong, the capital of Meghalaya, on September 21, 1980. It is one of the dialect community fellowships of the Kukis.

Most of the KWS units have diaspora Kukis, that is, Kukis who do not live on their ancestral land.

The various units of KWS are:

- KWS-Shillong
- KWS-Delhi
- KWS-Happy Valley
- KWS-Guwahati
- KWS-Bangalore
- KWS-Hyderabad/Secunderabad
- KWS-Kolkata
- KWS-Pune
- KWS-Chennai
- KWS-Itanagar
- KWS-Mumbai
- KWS-Silchar
- KWS-Aizawl

---

[61] *Thempu* is the priest of a village for humanity.

- KWS-Poducherry
- KWS-Dibrugarh

The units of KWS outside India are:

- KWS-Kuala Lumpur, Malaysia
- KWS-London, UK
- KWS-Yangon
- KWS-Singapore

Formed in 2002, All India Kuki Worship Service Coordinating Committee (AIKWSCC) is responsible for establishing relationships among the KWS units. It felicitates and nurtures the ministry of all the units as "Unity in KWS."

KWS focuses on the work of God as seen in Christ Jesus for Kuki humanity and salvation. It has adopted common logos and the theme *Shine for Christ*, which began with a personal value for those who *Live in Christ* or *Shine in Christ*. People who *Shine in Christ* reflectively *Shine for Christ* in corporate life to promote Kuki humanity and salvation. It has a formal structure but at the same time it is movement-oriented; it is traditional and yet innovative, exclusive and yet inclusive. The units of KWS are independent and have autonomous identities; and dynamic relationships prevail among them. KWS with its focus on community, God, internal care and external service is a non-denominational fellowship with an inter-denominational outlook.[62]

---

[62] Dino L. Touthang, *"Future Prospects of KWS"* Guwahati , Khanglai 2008 cum KWS-G Decade Celebration, Souvenir (October, 2008), 36-38.

Summary

This chapter focussed on the meaning of the term "Kuki" and Kuki unity in tradition, custom, culture, folklore, folktales and religion. It also looked at the positive role that Kuki Worship Service has been playing in binding people together through community worship. The chapter also focused on various KWS units and the main aim of KWS, which is to enable the Kuki community to shine in Christ for humanity and salvation.

CHAPTER TWO

Kuki Worship Service: A Study

Introduction

The term "Kuki Worship Service" means *Kukite Houkhawmna Natoh* in a local dialect of the people. They gather through the spirituality of worship-together called *Houkhawm* in the form of fellowship as a community people for humanity and salvation. Service (*natoh*) in the spirituality of Christ, the "True Son of the Holy-father God" called *Tahchapa-Jesu*, is the strength of the fellowship people of KWS. Therefore, the ministry of KWS is *Pathien Houkhawmna Natoh* (Pathien Hou Natohna), which means *Pathien Worship Service*, because Kuki people worship Holy Father God of above called *Chung Pathien*. The ministry of KWS focuses mainly on God as seen in Jesus Christ. It also focuses on the Kuki community.[1] The Spirit of God at work, which was manifested in the life, teaching and ministry of *Tahchapa-Jesu*, is the source of service in devotion to God for the growth and prosperity of Kuki humanity and salvation or liberation.

---

[1] Messianic People of God who believe in the person and works of Christ Jesus for humanity, growth, prosperity and freedom or salvation.

However, a denominational notion has been an ideological sprite of Christian made centrifugal force imposed for further division of community people in the name of doctrine and church organisations. It would be a wholistic redemption for humankind and the world if God as seen in Christ Jesus is not owned exclusively as a property of one religious group. The incarnation of the "Love of God" in Christ Jesus has been the centrifugal spirit behind making positive relationships among the Kukis, their neighbours and other creation.

There is a concern among the Kuki diaspora for coming together in the spirituality of Christ for humanity, salvation and growth. It is due to their awareness of being one conglomerate group and their subsequent quest to worship together in their own dialect in the midst of other large human communities.

This chapter focuses on the formation of Kuki Worship Service (KWS), which refers to both a KWS unit and all the KWS units put together.

Origin of Kuki Worship Service

Kuki Worship Service (KWS) was first started in Shillong, the capital of Meghalaya, on September 21, 1980. Many Kuki students in Shillong at that time felt the need for community people to get together in worship. Initially, under the aegis of the Kuki Students Organisation (KSO), Shillong, it was known as Kuki Students' Worship Service, Shillong (KSWS-S). The worship service functioned under the students' body. Kuki Students' Union, Shillong, founded in 1975, also functioned as a body meant for the care of students before the existence of KSO/KWS.

In 1982, KSWS-S became Kuki Worship Service, Shillong (KWS-S) in order to include family members in worship service and to facilitate their active participation. On May 6, 1986, a decision was taken to turn KSO and KWS into two separate autonomous bodies. KWS Shillong is now regarded as the founding unit.

The beginning of most of the other units of KWS, such as Delhi, Pune, Bangalore, Hyderabad, Guwahati, Kolkata and Mumbai, were similar to that of the KWS-Shillong, where students took the initiative. However, family parent initiates in some KWS units were formed recently, such as Happy Valley (Shillong), Itanagar, Silchar and Aizawl.

KWS was formed out of concern for community in the knowledge of God. With its human outlook, KWS opened the door for everyone by following the basic belief in God as seen in Christ for Kuki humanity, growth and salvation. The eternal work of God called *Pathien* 'Holy Father'[2] among humans in the person and spirit of Jesus Christ; his virgin birth and sinless life; his service for humanity and teachings, self sacrificial death and resurrection; justification of fallen man solely by the grace of God through faith in Christ; the indwelling believers work of Holy spirit; the resurrection of both the saved and the lost; the spiritual unity of humans in Jesus Christ and the Bible as the inspired Word of God, infallible and the Book of Human Documentation.[3]

Units of Kuki Worship Service (KWS) In India

KWS-Shillong (KWS-S)

With the formation of KWS-Shillong in 1982 as a body separate from KSWS, worship service was conducted at St. Edmunds

---

[2] For the Kuki people, God is primaly and traditionally known as the "Most High" and is known as *Chung Pathien*, which means "Holy Father, God of above."

[3] Dino L. Touthang, *Future prospect of KWS*, Guwahati, Khanglai 2008 cum *KWS-G Decade Celebration, Souvenir* (October 2008). 36

and St. Anthony's College. A church-building committee was formed in 1994, and a plot at Law-u-sib, Madanriting, Shillong, was purchased on December 8, 2003, for church building. While the construction of the church building was in progress, a room for worship was dedicated on January 30, 2005, by Pastor L. B. Angam.

There are eight prayer cells in KWS-Shillong, namely (1) Paniel (2) Bandstand (3) Nongthymmai (4) Immanuel (5) Nongrim Hills (6) Daniel (7) Nehemiah and (8) NEHU.

Rev. Jamkhosei Guite, sponsored by KWS-S, went for his BD study at UB, Pune, and after the completion of his course in 2006, served as Chaplain and later as Pastor. KWS-S is now sponsoring Thenmang Singson, who is pursuing his BD course at UBS, Pune, since 2010. KWS-S has also supported missionaries in partnership with Indian Campus Crusade for Christ (ICCC), Kuki Christian Church (KCC), Friends Missionary Prayer Band (FMPB) and Evangelical Congregation Church of India (ECCI).[4]

Activities of KWS-S
KWS-S takes care of:

- Revival meetings/crusade
- Vacation Bible School (VBS)
- Music training for members
- It's choir

KWS Shillong hosted Khanglai 2011 in collaboration with KWS-Happy Valley and Golden Jubilee of KSO, Shillong.

---

[4] Telephonic interview with Lalboi Gangte, General, Secretary, KWS Shillong, and Rev. Jamkhosei Guite, Pastor, KWS Shillong on 21.08.10 (8-9 a.m.).

Kuki Worship Service-Delhi *(KWS-D)*

KWS-Delhi (KWS-D) was formed in 1992 by committed students in consultation with elders and advisors of KSO, Delhi. The Secretary, Moral and Religion of KSO, Delhi, was given the responsibility to look after the spiritual needs of its members before the formation of KWS in Delhi. Consecration of the fellowship was held at St. Stephen Chapel administered by Ashong Singsit. Even though there was no ordained leader in the initial stages at different points of time, the void was filled by Stephen Haopu and later by Rev. Seikam Touthang. As devoted leaders, Stephen Haopu and Seikam Touthang shared the word of God and, at times, leaders of other fellowships were invited according to need. The first KWS-D Executive Committees had: Chairman Tongminthang Haokip, Vice-Chairman Janglun Singson, Secretary Haokhosei Haokip, Joint Secretary Lhunkhosei Mate (Seipa), Finance Secretary Neikhol Haolai, Treasurer Ms. Boinu Sitlhou and Information Secretary Haokholal Haokip.[5]

Main Aims and Objectives of KWS-Delhi

- To administer the spiritual needs of its members in the context of minority community living in the midst of diverse cultures — secular as well as religious.

- To promote the spiritual well-being and communitarian unity; to protect the fraternal integrity of its members and to preserve the interdenominational character of the fellowship.

- To foster a learning community and a thinking fellowship to engage in the social issues and concerns that affect its members and society as a whole

---

[5] Lutngam Singson, *KWSD in the last ten years* (*Ebenezer*: Decade Celebration Souvenir 1992-9002) 7 and 8.

- To be a fellowship that is engaged in proclaiming the Gospel of Jesus Christ and spreading his message of salvation, freedom and eternal life.[6]

KWS-D Chaplain

The arrival of Dino L. Touthang and his family in the last quarter of 1995 and his subsequent induction as Chaplain of KWS-D marked a new beginning in the history of the fellowship. The fellowship experienced a new thrust and has been growing under his spiritual leadership. Letlal Haokip was inducted as Assistant Chaplain on April 1, 2002. He was ordained for the ministry by Kuki Baptist Convention (KBC) on February 6, 2007.

Activities of KWS-D

The first Prayer Cell was set up on January 10, 1997, at Nehru Vihar, North Campus of Delhi University, and a Bible camp was conducted at Mount Carmel School for the first time in 1990. KWS-D hosted the first *Khanglai*, an All India Kuki Worship Service Conference, from October 26-30, 2002. KWS-D has so far sent five volunteers for "Care Force Ministry" in United Kingdom.

KWS-D has performed several spiritual and social activities, such as Evangelistic Week, annual Medical Camp in the slums of Delhi in partnership with Deeper Life Ministry, Care and Concern Ministry in collaboration with Kuki Women Union in Manipur, the first *Family Camp 2009*, Career Guidance Seminar in collaboration with Kuki Students Organisation, Delhi, All India Prayer Fellowship during September 2009, *Mission Sunday* on every second Sunday of July and giving out small tokens of appreciation to some of the fellowship members who are working in different ministries or having their own

---

[6] *Ibid.*, 36.

ministry in Delhi. KWS-D has also started working in the slum in East Delhi; it gives education through tuition, Self Help Groups (SHG), medical camp, health awareness programmes and so on.[7]

Kuki Worship Service-Happy Valley (KWS-HV)

Formation and Growth

The Kuki Worship Service-Happy Valley (KWS-HV) unit was founded on April 7, 1997. The members are mostly military pensioners' family living in their own home, students and other workers. The objectives of KWS-HV are similar to those of other units of KWS. It currently includes more than 100 families with more than 500 registered members.

KWS-HV purchased its own Church plot on September 15, 2005. The construction of the church building is in progress. Rev. Seiminthang Chongloi was appointed to minister as Pastor in 2008. KWS-HV is sponsoring Rev. K. Hutoi Achumi as a missionary worker in collaboration with FMPB and Ms. Mary Khawlboi Lenthang as missionary in collaboration with ECCI, Manipur. The different administrative departments of KWS Happy Valley are: Missionary Board, Church Building Committee, Women Society, Youth Fellowship and Children Sunday School Department.[8]

Kuki Worship Service-Guwahati (KWS-G)

KWS-Guwahati was formed under the care of KSO Guwahati leaders, particularly Alet Doungel (President). In the initial stages, responsibility of worship service was shouldered by KSO (G). Later, a resolution was passed at the residence of V.

---

[7] Letlal Haokip, Pastor, KWS Delhi; personal mail to the author, 4th August 2010.

[8] Lutngam Singson, *KWSD in the last ten years* (Ebenezer; Decade Celebration Souvenir 1992-9002) 7 and 8.

Changsan for a dedication service. Dedication of worship was held at Satribati Christian Hospital Chapel on January 4, 1998. Seventy-three members were present on the day of formation. At present, the fellowship service has more than 400 members. KSO-G handed over the responsibility of worship service to the congregation the people's meeting held on October 9, 1998. The drafted constitution of KWS (G) was amended on April 7, 2002. At present, Rev. M. Haokhothong is ministering the people as Pastor. Youth Department, Women Department, Church Building Committee and Missionary Board are some of the bodies under KWS G.[9] KSO-G handed over the responsibility of worship service to the people in the people's meeting on October 9, 1998. The following persons were elected as Executive Committee KWS-G: Rev. M Haokhothong, Chairman/Pastor; Gl Helun Hangsing, Secretary; Ng. Nengpi Lhouvum, Assistant Secretary; and Ms. Nemboi Manchong, Finance Secretary and Treasurer.

Activities of KWS-G

KWS (G) Missionary works supported Evan Thomas Limbu (Nepali Church, Maligaon) in 1998 and other missionaries in 2002. It maintains joint fellowship with her own people, Hmar Worship service and Zomi Christian Fellowship (ZCF). KWS-G does mission work: It gave donation to FMPB in 2004. It has also been supporting some missionaries for Gospel preaching in Guwahati since 2006. In addition, KWS-G organised *Huhhingna Camp* in 1999. *Decade Celebration* and *Khanglai 2008* were organised by AIKWSCC during October 9-12, 2008.[10] The

---

[9] Lunjalen Khongsai, *Ten Yeasr of Glorious Walk with God*, Guwahati, Khanglai 2008 cum KWS-G *Decade Celebration, Souvenir*, (October, 2008). 40-44

[10] Personal telephonic interview with Pa Lunjalen Khongsai, August 19, 2010.

Church Building Committee was formed on January 30, 2000. The construction of the church building on Chachal VIP Road, 6th Mile Area, was dedicated on October 3, 2010.

Youth Department (Khanglaite)

KWS (G) Youth Department was founded on March 12, 2006, with the theme "Let your light so shine" (Matt 5:16). The responsibility for looking after Sunday school was given to the youth department. It conducts Bible Quiz and celebrates Children Day and the like. The KWS (G) Choir was formed in 2008. It also conducts Music Fest and Youth Day called *Khanglai* and seminars on themes like motivation and discipleship. In addition, it produces Gospel albums and visits the other KWS units in Shillong.[11]

Women Department (Nupite)

KWS (G) Women department was founded on January 4, 1998. During the year of formation, prayer for obtaining a plot for church building, church construction and the like were its main concerns. *Nupite* helps the church in making its furniture; it also supports missionaries.[12]

Kuki Worship Service-Bangalore (KWS-B)

The resolution to form worship service in Bangalore was made by theologians and KSO leaders of Bangalore on July 2, 1999. The first worship service was held at Bangalore Bible Church No. 435, Bangalore. The worship service named the fellowship as KWS-Bangalore. The following were selected as its executive members: S. Obed Haokip, Chaplain; Thonglunminthang, Secretary; Khamkhosiam Simte and Hatneichong. Members; President and Secretary KSO-Bangalore, ex-officio.

---

[11] KWS(G), *Church Inauguration Souvenir* (Guwahati: KWS-G 2010) 64-73.

[12] *Ibid.,* 71.

KWS-B came across a kind of instability at the end of 2000 due to the resignation of the Chaplain and going away of some of the students after completion of their academic course. However, in 2002, Mangcha Haokip from UTC, various theological seminary students and KSO joined hands and revived the worship service. The fellowship, which had 15-20 members in the initial stage, currently has about 450 members.

Activities of KWS-B

Various local Prayer Cells were formed at Austin Town, Indira Nagar and Lingarajpuram. Sunday school and Woman fellowship are the departments that function under KWS-B. A plot for the construction of the church building has been purchased and the fellowship currently publishes a monthly Magazine called *Lhagao Thimthu*.[13]

Kuki Worship Service-Hyderabad (KWS-H)

The need for establishing worship for the Kukis living in the city of Hyderabad, Andhra Pradesh, was fulfilled with the initiation of Daniel Hangsing and T. Changsan. Nengpi Singson, who runs *Widow Home Ministry*, used to have fellowship with the youths without any formal name for the fellowship. A resolution was made in the fellowship meeting that was held at the residence of Daniel Singson on March 7, 1999, to organise the participants as KWS-H. It came to be officially known as KWS. The following persons were elected as executive members: Thomjakhup Changsan, Chairman; Niangpi Singson, Secretary; Chinbiakhoi Singson, Treasurer; Lunminthang Kipgen and Daniel Singson, members.

Prayer Cells of four different colonies, namely A. G. Colony, Sainikpuri, Banjara Hills and Alwal, have been functioning with

---

[13] James Kipgen, *KWS Bangalore History* (Bangalore: Decade Celebration Souvenir ,1999-2009) 14-17

the active participation of the youths. A monthly bulletin called *Charizma* is published under the care of the Executive Board. This bulletin was first brought out in 2006. The worship service is conducted at Centenary Baptist Church, Secunderabad. Senior Pastor Rev. Nalla Thomas allowed the Kukis in Hyderabad to worship there for more than seven years without any charge of rent because of his love, care and concern for the Kukis. KWS-H celebrated its decennium in 2009.[14]

Kuki Worship Service-Kolkata (KWS-K)

The need for the formation of worship service for Kuki people in Kolkata was initiated by family parents and KSO leaders. A meeting was held at the residence of Lamthang Singsit at Dumdum Airport on August 26, 2001. The meeting resolved to form a fellowship as Kuki Worship Service-Kolkata (KWS-K), with the appointment of a chairman, a secretary and a treasurer. The following persons were chosen and entrusted with leading responsibilities:Tongkholun Haokip, Chairman; Sehkhokai Singson, Secretar:; Rev. Daniel Darlong, Chaplain; and Pastor Biaka Vaiphei Treasurer; later, Miss. Tingjalhing Lhouvum was appointed as Treasurer and Mary Chinkholhing continued.

The inaugural programme of KWS-Kolkata was held at the residence of L. Singsit on September 9, 2001, followed by a feast of solemnity. More than 35 members attended the first worship service. The KWS-Kolkata fellowship meeting began to be conducted at United Pentecostal Church, 25/1 Pullin Pally Dumdum. Later, place of worship was shifted to Colinga Baptist Church, 46 Ripon Street, Kolkata-16.[15]

---

[14] T. Changsan, *KWS Hung kuphudoh thusim chomcha* (Hyderabad: Decade Souvenir, 1999-2009) 9-10 and Henginlen Kipgen, *KWS-H Thusim* (Hyderabad: Decade Souvenir, 1999-2009) 3-5.

[15] Interview with Biaka Vaiphei, Field Secy, UPC Kolkata on September 19, 2010, and narrated by Haojakhup Kipgen, Chairman, KWS-Kolkata in addition to KWS-K Secretary record book.

Activities of KWS-Kolkata

At the initial stage, KWS-Kolkata began its worship service on every first Sunday of the month. Later, it was rescheduled for every second and fourth Sunday of the month under the chairmanship of Haojakhup Kipgen.

The arrival of Paul Paolen and his ordination followed by initiation as Pastor changed the frequency of worship. Regular Sunday worship service started in August 2009. Through his initiation, a "Song Book" of praise and worship was published. KWS-Kolkata took a resolution to support Mr. Thangboi for future ministry. With positive anticipation of our request to AIKWSCC leaders, KWS-London, initiated to sponsor him for a four-year BD course at Bishop's College, Kolkata. Since its inception, KSO has been functioning as a founding youth department for KWS (K). Ushering of worship service and taking care of the property is KSO's responsibility.[16] KWS-Kolkata is currently celebrating its tenth year of God's graceful leading.

During 2009, Sunday school under the voluntary care of Nu Boinu and Didim took good care of children at KWS (K). Children were taught Bible verses and songs and other activities were carried out according to the arrangement of teachers.[17]

Kuki Worship Service-Pune (KWS-P)

A get-together meeting was held for all the Kukis residing in Pune on August 26, 1995, at Alliance Church under the visionary initiation of Stephen Touthang and the like. This meeting marked the beginning of KSO and KWS in Pune.

---

[16] KWS-K Secretary Record: General Meeting (Colinga Baptist Church on 23/8/2006) Resolution No. 3 and 23.9.06 resolution. Also narrated by Seiminlen (Jempu Haokip) Secy. KWS Kolkata 2010.

[17] *Ibid.,* Resolution No.10.

Worship service was conducted on alternate Sundays for around 30 members. A worship leader used to be appointed to look after the worship service until the full-fledged executive body of KWS-Pune was formed in 2003. KWS-Pune currently conducts regular Sunday worship service in the Church of Holy Name, CNI, at Guru Warpath.

Activities of KWS-Pune

- **Prayer Cell:** There are six prayer cells: Kondhwa, Camp Area, Sanghvi, Ghorpadi, Quarter Gate and Bibvewadi. Members of KWS meet here to study, share and pray together as "Prayer Cell" groups.

- **Shom-Inn Ministry:** Celebration of KWS-Pune in 2005 marked a progressive change to start a boy's hostel, traditionally known as SHOM-INN. A "Discipleship Centre" was established. It became the most important ministry of the fellowship to impart "ways of life" according to the teaching of Christ.

- **Sports Ministry:** It functions as one of the most interesting ministries where sports is used as a means to reach out to young people within and outside the fellowship.[18]

- Sunday school for kids, hospital visits, support missionaries, spiritual campus, crusade, retreat and project for purchasing vehicle are in progress.

Kuki Worship Service-Chennai (KWS-C)

The first fellowship of the Kukis in Chennai was held at Sosom's resident, St. Thomas Mount, in 2003. In the following year, Eimi Association Chennai (EAC) was formed as "Social Welfare" at

---

[18] Thongkhotinlal and Hemkhomang, *Kuki Worship Service Pune* Guwahati, Khanglai 2008 cum KWS-G Decade Celebration, Souvenir (October, 2008). 78.

Gurukul Theological College. The first prayer meeting of Eimi Christian Fellowship Chennai (ECFC) was held at Ngailien's residence, Choolaimedu, as cottage prayer meeting on September 10, 2005. In 2008, there arose a proposal to change ECFI into Kuki Worship Service-Chennai.

Many felt the need for the formation of KWS. During December 2008, an Advent Christmas programme was proposed for which KWS-Bangalore was invited. Under the leadership of D.P. Haokip, Vice Chairman of AIKWSCC, accompanied by more than twenty members of KWS-Bangalore, attended the programme. ECFC was rechristened as Kuki Worship Service-Chennai (KWS-C) in consultation with ECFC leaders on December 7, 2008, under the initiation of Parents.[19]

The first administrative body of KWS-C (2009-2010) consisted of Pastor Lalboy Haokip (Chaplaincy), Pa. Mangboi Lhungdim (Chairman), Gl. Lal Moyah Greendy Vaiphei (General Secretary), Gl. Mangminlen Vaiphei and Gl. Lelen Kipgen (Joint Secretary), Gl. Lalzawm Gangte and Gl. Lulun Haokip (Music Secretary), Kimshi Lhungdim and Bebem Vaiphei (Assistant Music Secretary), Hegou Chongloi (Finance Secretary), Hoineikim Singson (Treasurer) and Paul , Seiboi, Hahao, Lucy, Joujam, Boinu, Doihkim and Phaphal (Ushers).

- **Women Ministry:** Nu. Chongneo Haokip (Chairperson), Nu. Grace Haokip (Secretary) and Nu Lalam Lhungdim (Treasurer)

- **Sunday School Department:** Pa Ginlenthang Guite (Superintendent) and Ng. Kimshi Lhungdim (Assistant Superitendent)

- **Advisors:** Pa. Ginlenthang Guite and Pa. Thangpao Haokip

---

[19] Mangboi Lhungdim, Chairman, KWS-Chennai; mail to the author, August 10, 2010.

Activities of KWS-Chennai

Lalboi Haokip was appointed as Pastor of KWS-C. Sunday Worship Services are held at Salvation Army Church, Puruwakam. It opened Prayer Cells in different colonies. KWS-C offers financial assistance in emergencies to its members and helps sick members. Women Ministry was formed to help women solve their problems. The Sunday school department is meant for teaching Bible verses and songs to children.[20]

Kuki Worship Service-Mumbai (KWS-M)

One of the first get-togethers *(Lenkhawm)* and marriage celebrations of Chongboi Doungel with Lunthang Haokip was organised by Clay Khongsai at his residence at Kailash Apartments in 1995. Gradually, these get-togethers became an annual affair and the tradition of annual "Social Cum Worship Service Meet" grew. With this, there has been a widespread awareness of the need for a platform to worship together in their own mother tongue, preferably in the form of Kuki Worship Service (KWS) as done in other cities. An opinion poll was conducted whether to start Kuki Worship Service in Mumbai or not on September 6, 2008. A majority of the people on that day voted for the formation of KWS-M, and so there arose in principle approval for the establishment of KWS-M.

Activities of KWS-M

Under the aegis of KSO (M), President Mangboi Mate and General Secretary Neopu Lhouvum organised worship service cum Christmas celebrations on 25th December 2008. On that day, they decided to conduct the first KWS (M) worship service, which was eventually held on January 18, 2009. The first Kuki

---

[20] Lalboi Haokip, Pastor KWS Chenna, mail to the author, August 14, 2010).

Worship Service-Mumbai meeting was held at Gyan Ashram, Andheri (E), under the aegis of KSO(M), led by Mangneo Haokip (Chairman, YWAM). With a lot of introspection, the congregation of the first KWS (M) met and prayed to the Almighty. The first meet turned out to be better than expected and an executive committee was formed on May 30, 2009. An Executive Committee of the KWS (M) was formed at the residence of T. Lhungdim in Mumbai: T. Lhungdim (Chairman), Jangchon Lhouvum (Secretary), Lunkhongam Haokip (Finance Secretary) and Mangneo Haokip (Chaplain).

KWS-M currently conducts regular worship service in the first and third week of every month at Gyan Ashram, Andheri (East). As of now, about 40-50 members attend the services regularly—to put on record that God has brought thus far and the Spirit will carry the future according to His will.[21]

Kuki Worship Service-Itanagar (KWS-I)

The formation of KWS-Itanagar (KWS-I) was declared by Dr. T. Lhungdim with prayer of dedication by Rev. Satlhun Hangsing on 12th October 2008. It was formed under the initiation of family parents and other government employees, businesspersons and a few students. It may be noted that no student's organisation of the Kukis was behind the formation of KWS in Itanagar.

The KWS fellowship of Itanagar has around 40 members and is currently growing. Committee members have been appointed to take care of initiative administration, and area representatives have also been selected.[22] The first KWS Itanagar committee members included Dr. Thensei Lhungdim

---

[21] T. Lhungdim, Leader KWS-Mumbai, letter to the author, July 27, 2010.

[22] Telephonic interview with Asat Hangsing, Pastor, KWS-Itanagar, October 28, 2010.

(Chairman), Rev. Mangkholal Kipgen (Secretary), Mrs. Themboi Kipgen (Treasurer) and Kamkhogin Vaiphei and Lelen Haokip (Church Elders). Haolenmang Haokip from Itanagar Area, Mangboi Kipgen from Nahar Lagun area and Seiboi Kipgen from Nirjuli and Doimukh Area were area representatives.

Kuki Worship Service-Silchar (KWS-S)

A cottage prayer meeting was held in Silchar, Assam, before the formation of KWS. Bro. Letkai Simte, Seilal Doungel, Ms. Marykim Haokip, Pauthang Haokip and the like took initiative in the fellowship prayer meeting. There was a proposal to name the fellowship after a month of prayer meetings. The decision to christen the fellowship as Kuki Worship Service-Silchar was taken on August 23, 2009. The following persons were chosen as Executive Members: Kamchon Chongloi (Chairman), Ms Kimting Singson (Vice Chairperson), Seilal Doungel (Secretary), Ms Nengpi Thangeo (Assistant Secretary) and Ms Chongvah Doungel (Treasurer/Finance Secretary).

So, KWS-Silchar was formed at New Testament Baptist Church Hall, Silchar. Sunday worship services are conducted there at 2:00 p.m. Apart from Sunday worship service, occasions like Christmas, Good Friday, Foundation Day, etc., are observed under the initiation of Rev. Jamkhosei Guite. KWS-Silchar is currently processing an application to the Government of Assam to provide land for the church building and administration.[23]

---

[23] Telephonic Interview with Kamchon Chongloi, Chairman, KWS-Silchar, August 21, 2010.

Kuki Worship Service-Aizawl *(KWS-A)*

As mentioned in the previous chapter, "Mizo" is also a term used to refer to Kukis in the twentieth-century. People of Aizawl are originally "Kukis" but politically "Mizo" from the movement of Mizoram and attainment of statehood in 1987. Lushai, a Kuki clan people, built the Aizawl hill city. However, people belonging to one dialect group need to get together to know each other better.

With this in mind, a kind of meeting was held in March 2010. After deliberating on the matter for some time, it was decided that worship service would be done on the second and last Sunday of every month. Subsequently, KWS-Aizawl was formed and the first service was held on 11th April 2010. KWS-Aizawl is an interdenominational worship service that aims at ministering the word of God to needy souls and building better relationships among the Kukis and their own people, the Aizawlian. It is still growing and hopes to be used by God to move His Kingdom forward. The following are Committee Members of KWS Aizawl:[24] Chairman, Shokhothang Haokip; V. Chairman, Letkhoneh Haokip; Secretary, Letkholun Haokip; Finance Secretary; Haopu Doungel; and Treasurer, H. D. Lunkhosei.

Kuki Worship Service-Pondicherry (KWS-P)

KWS-Pondicherry formally started on 28th August 2011. The purpose of KWS-P is to cater for spiritual need and to offer service to the community in all possible ways. Whether they have everything or whether they are in need, KWS wants to make people understand the good news of God's love bringing happiness, forgiveness and a new life in Christ Jesus.

---

[24] Sokhothang Haokip, "KWS Aizawl: Brief Sketch" (August 13, 2010), personal mail to the author (August 14, 2010) and telephonic interview with him on August 18, 2010.

Pu Manglen Singson Inn (Pondicherry University) is the place of worship for Sunday worship service. The following persons have been appointed as leaders for KWS-P: Rev. Paolen (Paul) Haokip (Pastor), Gl. Khupminthang Hangsing (Secretary), Ng. Lhingpineng (Pipi) Thangeo (Treasurer) and Thangminlun Khongsai (Information. Secretary).[25]

Kuki Worship Service-Dibrugarh

The Kuki Inter-denominational Christian Church (KICC) of Dibrugarh, Assam, celebrated its second Advent Christmas on 9th November 2011 and unanimously changed KICC into Kuki Worship Service-Dibrugarh (KWS-D). The visit for All India Kuki Worship Service Co-Ordination Committee (AIKWSCC) was fixed for Sunday, 20th November 2011. The following persons were elected as leaders: Chairman, L.Doungel; Vice-Chairman, Hauthang Kilong; Secretary, Paolien Chongloi: Asst. Secretary, Gigin Haokip; Finance Secretary, Lulun Gangte; Treasurer, Chinneo Chongloi; Newsletter Board:Haopu Kipgen Khukhup Hangzo, Sangboi Doungel and John Lupheng.[*]

KWS Abroad

KWS in Kuala Lumpur *(KWS-KL)*

With the formation of Kuki Students Democratic Front (KSDF), Kuala Lumpur, on September 10, 2005, the need to organise prayer fellowship was sharply felt. As a result, a fellowship named "Kuki Worship Service-Kuala Lumpur" was formed.

---

[25] Khupminthang Hangsing, "KWS-Pondicherry: Resolution of their meeting", *FELLOWSHIP THU.. Fellowship hi akiman na asot tan hijeh ah chun Formalise bolding thu akisei khom min akikhom chengsen nopto na akinei tan ahi. Fellowship minsah ding akiseijin,mipi nop dungjui jin KUKI WORSHIP SERVICE PONDICHERRY kiti dingin akiki houlhatai and Rev. Paul Paolen's facebook.*

[*] *kwsnet@yahoogroups.com* 17 November 2011 13:46

The following persons were chosen as its executive members: Let sei (Chairman), Gin Son Mang (Ginsonmang) (Secretary) and Pastor Hesei Touthang (Chaplain). The executive members were appointed by the leading founder P.S. Haokip. KWS-KL conducts its worship service at KSDF Office.

Kuki Worship Service in London *(KWS-L)*

KWS-London was founded on July 8, 2007, at St. George Church, East Ham. KWS-L is an inter-denominational Christian fellowship founded for the Kuki diaspora community living in London and around United Kingdom. Its main purpose is to reach out to and support the Kuki community in Diaspora with the love of God and fellowship and prayer based on biblical principles and practices. The objective is to promote the spiritual and physical well-being of members and to proclaim the gospel of Jesus Christ, spreading his message of love, salvation, freedom and eternal life.[26]

After the initiation of Lien Gangte and Nenghoi, who were active members of KWS Delhi, they approached Rev. David Haokip, Vicar of St. George, East Ham. They held the first service at The Vicarage, Buxton Road, East Ham, London. Thirteen members attended the first service on Sunday, July 8, 2007, in which Pi Kim Telien was the speaker. The executive members of KWS–London are: Rev. Canon David (Tongkhoyam) Haokip (Chairman), Chonminlien (Lien) Gangte (Secretary) and Neihlam Vaiphei Gerbaldi (Treasurer).[27]

KWS-London holds its prayer meetings in London on every second Sunday. It also celebrates Kut Festival and Christmas. Since its inception, KWS-London has been sponsoring

---

[26] *www.kwslondon.com (06-08-2011)*

[27] Chonminlen Gangte, Secy. KWS-London, letter to the author, July 28, 2010.

Thangboi (Ngamkhothang) to study BD at Bishop's College, Kolkata, in support of AIKWSCC leaders' information for KWS-Kolkata and future ministry.

Kuki Community Church in Tulsa *(USA)*

For the past ten years, the Kuki people in USA have been getting together for worship functions in the name of Asian Baptist Church at Tulsa, Oklahoma. Ever since worship at functions started to be performed in the local dialect the number of members has risen. So, the Annual Assembly held on December 26, 2010, had a prolonged discussion about changing the name of the get-together church. A resolution was adopted, and the name of Asian Baptist Church was changed into Kuki Community Church.[28]

Kuki Worship Service-Yangon *(KWS-Y)*

The Kuki Worship Service-Yangon (KWS-Y) was formed on June 25, 2011, at Yangon, Myanmar. It is an inter-denominational fellowship of the *Pathien Houkhawm* community. It is a get-together fellowship of the Kuki people attending worship service in different denominational church organisations in the city and around Yangon.[29]

---

[28] Lalam Touthang, *"min kikhelta (name change)"*, Kukiforum Tuesday, January 25, 2011

[29] Personal letter to the author by Yampao; Advisor, KWS-Yangon. July 26, 2011. *Dear Thangboi, Dam a nakimanchah jing kahet jieh in Pathienkathangvah ie. KWS Yangon thu lunglutna nasatah nanei jieh in kipa aum ie. KWS Yangon, ahung kiphudohna ajieh chu Yangon a um denomination chomchom a um eimiho jousen eimapao a Pathienhoukhom theina dinga Fellowship dinmun a hungkiphutdoh ahibouvie. Tutua hi lhakhat a khatve (last week of the month) Fellowship houkhom kinei ahin, nungleh aphatdungjui a khintou toudinga ngaito ahi. Hitobanghi Yangon dinmun a hungvat tahjieh a kiphutdoh bou ahin, muntin a KWS houkhom aumvanga kiphutdoh jong ahideh sampoi. Na email kamu nia pet KWS Yangon Secretary pu kom nangchu mail naboldinga kaseiahin, nahinthot jou hitadin katahsan e. Hungpon thon, Keima napa Pau*

The executive committee of KWS-Yangon consists of: Yam Kho Pau and Thong Kho Thang (Advisors), Ot Kho Thang (Chaplain), Htong Hlun (Assistant Chaplain), LunNeh (Secretary), Rev. Pao Kho Lal (Joint Secretary), Lhing Ja Lam (Ngahnu) (Treasurer) and Syama Mong Nei Vah (Accountant). Its members include: Neh Kho Lal, Kam Kho Thang, Ngam Kho Sei, Hao Jang, Chin Kho Neng, Hat Kho Neng, Lun Kho Ngam, Kai Kho Let, Jam Kho Len and Zam Kho Lal.[30]

Kuki Worship Service in Singapore

Kuki Worship Service in Singapore was inaugurated on November 6, 2011. The following members were elected to the unit committee: Neh Kho Sei (Chairman), Neng Bul (Secretary) and Kikim (Treasurer).*

Newly Expected Units of KWS

KWS fellowship of Bawm and others in Dhaka, Bangladesh, is deliberating on its formal inauguration. The Kukis of Mandalay, Myanmar, are willing to be part of KWS Worldwide.[31]

---

[30] Personal letter to the author by Lun Neh; Secy. KWS-Yangon. August 3, 2011. *Dear Nkthang, Greetings from KWS-Yangon! "KWS-Yangon thusim" thu chu ka hin thot ding ahi. Yangon(Myanmar) hi Khopi khat a hi in, masang a pan a Eimi te ho a na chen apat, Yangon Eimi Fellowship tia kikhop na ki nei jin ahi. (Lha khat a vei khat) Thu jat chom chom ho jeh in Fellwoship bol lou in a naum in ahi. Tu kum May 14th chung Rev. Ot Kho Thang in organized bol na toh Yangon a um Ojaho, Rev. Dr. Yam Kho Pau (AGS of Myanmar Councils of Churches) ina, kihou lim na khat a naum thei in ahi. Chu va kon chun Interdenominational fellowship nei ding lung gel a hung um doh in, International level a jong network nei thei na ding in KUKI WORSHIP SERVICE YANGON ti in ki form doh ahi e. Tu term kum a EC ho chu attached file toh ka hin thot e. Keima Lun Neh*

* *kwsnet@yahoogroups.com.* 19 November 2011 23:26

[31] David T. Haokip, *Golden Jubilee Souvenir 1961-2011, Kuki Students Organisation Shillong,* (Department of Publication) p. 95

All India Kuki Worship Service Coordinating Committee (AIKWSCC)

All India Kuki Worship Service Coordinating Committee (AIKWSCC) was formed on November 24, 2002, at the EFICOR office in New Delhi in the presence of some of the leaders of KWS units and members of Kuki Christian Leaders Fellowship (KCLF). The main aims and objectives of AIKWSCC are to coordinate various units of KWS for spiritual growth. It means to facilitate ministry of KWS through coordinative consultation, leadership seminars, closer interactions and exchange of ideas in developing joint projects, common constitution, motto and logo for the ministry of KWS.[32] Camps and conference are organised and other coordinative ideas are shared according to the need for the growth of KWS.[33]

Members of the first executive committee of AIKWSCC are: Rev. Dino L Touthang (Chairman), Pu J Lhungdim (Vice Chairman), Rev. Paothang Haokip (Secretary), (Lamboi) Rev. Jangkholam Haokip (Joint Secretary) and Pu LL Khongsai (Finance Secretary). In the executive meetings of Khanglai 2008 Guwahati, Pa Jangkholal Gangte (Lalboi) and Pu D.P. Haokip were elected as new Joint Secretary and Vice Chairman, respectively, in replacement.

A member or leader representing a KWS Unit is automatically a member of the organisation through the unit to which he or she belongs.

---

[32] Touthang, *op.cit.*, 37.

[33] Telephonetic interview with Lalboi Gangte, Joint Secy., AIKWSCC, 21/08/10 and with Paothang, Secy, AIKWSCC, 17/08/10 in addition to the drafted and un-amended constitution of AIKWSCC.

Summary

This chapter focused on the formation and growth of Kuki Worship Service. It also looked at the various units of Kuki Worship Service in India and abroad and the important activities they provide. We also looked at All India Kuki Worship Service Coordinating Committee (AlKWSCC) and its aims and objectives. Also, we learnt that a major part of KWS began with the initiation of students; therefore, it is also known as a "Student's Movement" (in the fear of God) for wisdom and for Kuki humanity and prosperity. The parents and guardians who took initiative to form KWS units were pre-inspired people.

CHAPTER THREE

Kuki Worship Service: A Unifying and Transforming Factor

Introduction

The purpose of this research is to investigate whether KWS functions as a unifying and transforming factor in Kuki society. This chapter aims to find a tangible view for analysing and interpreting the data acquired through empirical investigation. This chapter is based on the study of the collective information about the formation, growth and functions of the KWS units mentioned in the previous chapter. This chapter also looks at unity among the Kukis and transformation of their community. It also includes the inferences drawn from the empirical study carried out among KWS leaders and members of Eastern India.

Delineation of Unity and Transformation

Lenkhawm (get together) for the common purpose of belief or ideology or action in a shared situation is unity. It is used in the sense of harmony within a community people. Psalm 133:1 celebrates the beauty of brothers living "in unity."[1] It is also

---

[1] Hebr. *ýgam-y¹µa¼ý; ýyaµa¼ ý* means "together" and *ýgam ý*adds emphasis. Gk. *ýhenótȼsý*

interpreted as celebration of the fellowship *(houkhawm)* of the covenant community and celebration of the fellowship of the pilgrims.

God, the "above holy father" called *Chung Pathien*, is a term used to denote "self-existence being." The unity of *Chung Pathien* is argued from its self-existence, independence, perfection of its nature, omnipotence and unity of design in the works of nature[2] in the Kuki context. Unity in the theological sense signifies oneness of sentiment, affection, or behaviour (Ps 133:1). The "unity of the faith" is an equal belief of the same great truths of God and the possession of the grace of faith in a similar form and degree (Eph 4:13). The "unity of the spirit" is the union between Christ and his saints by which the same divine spirit dwells in both and having the same spirit dwell in them with holiness, faith, hope, love and care in Christ.[3]

Transformation

Kukis need to understand the value and quality of their way of life, which is unification for societal transformation. Transformation may also be understood as an act of changing form, shape or appearance. It is dependent upon the internal process "the renewal of your mind" and is paralleled by the person's differentiation from "the world" (Rom 12:2). It distinguishes the present hope in Christ from that which was

---

[2] McClintock and Strong Encyclopedia, *Electronic Database.* (Biblesoft Inc. 2000, 2003, 2005, 2006) by the doctrine was lost sight of by heathens, and maintained by Israel and in the Gospel. The Scriptures make no attempt to *prove* the doctrine, but assert it unequivocally. See Ex 20:3; Deut 4:35; 6:4; Ps 86:10; 1 Cor 8:4, 6, etc. When the doctrine of the Trinity (q.v.) was formulated, it became necessary for the Church to declare that this does not come into conflict with the doctrine of its unity. See also Hagenbach, *Hist. of Doct.* 1, 102, 330; Van Oosterzee, *Christian Dogmatics*, 1, 250

[3] McClintock and Strong Encyclopedia, *Electronic Database* (Biblesoft Inc. 2000, 2003, 2005, 2006).

available with the "old covenant" under Moses (2 Cor. 3:12-18). This transformation is described in both imperative terms (Rom 12: If.) and indicative passive terms, as that which is done for people of faith in Christ Jesus (2 Cor. 3:18).[4]

An Empirical Study on Unity and Transformation

This empirical investigation aims at ascertaining whether KWS functions as an unifying and transforming factor. It is an empirical data result based on the investigation carried out among KWS leaders and members. The main concern is to find out how leaders and members understand the role of KWS in unifying the Kukis and transforming their community. This sample includes data collected through interaction with 30 leaders and 69 members for analysing the findings of the research.

These respondents are leaders and members of KWS in Shillong, Happy Valley, Guwahati and Kolkata. The leaders are mostly government servants and the members are mostly students and others. Theologically trained people perform the ministerial function, while others are involved in administration. All of them meet together in KWS as a fellowship of worshipping community in Christ.

KWS Leaders' Response to the Question of Unity

On the role of KWS, 90 per cent of people's common notion and agreement shows that KWS is playing a unifying and transformative role. The respondents stated that the formation of the KWS in diaspora has helped people to forget denominational ways of worship at home. They opined that the few scattered people groups need to take care of themselves

---

4 Wm. B. Eerdmans, *International Standard Bible Encyclopedia*, (1979: Publishing Co.) revised edition.

according to their way of life, when they are in the midst of largely populated city people.

In contrast, 10 per cent of the people had a negative view. The respondents maintained that KWS is confined only to one dialect group and not the Kukis as a whole. They are critical of the pre-existence of other fellowship organisations in the name of tribe-dialects groups like Zomi Christian Fellowship, Hmar Fellowship, etc.

What can be a theological model for unity?

On the question of a theological model for unity, 63.63 per cent of the people supported the idea of "Universality of Christ" for creation as the preferred theological model for unity. The respondents opined that "Universality of Christ" is for all humankind. They stated that Christ as the light of the world is manifested in every way of life in a community. The way, truth and life seen in Christ Jesus nurture all aspects of life, not only the religious aspect.

Also, 15.15 per cent of the respondents stated that universality of Christ or the exclusive statement of faith and inclusiveness do not bother them. Another 15.15 per cent stood for exclusive statement of faith for unity because they regarded the exclusive model as a bond of unity. Only 6.06 per cent of the respondents feel that the inclusive theological model for unity will help all dialect groups of Kukis to achieve oneness — the oneness that stems from belonging to one community.

What could be an approach to unity?

On the question of approach to unity, 36.11 per cent prefer religious tolerance as the right approach. The respondents feel that religiosity as something "Christian" is a way to unity. Some of the respondents said that the *Khankho* "way of life" in which love, respect and obedience form the basis of ethical duty is a nurturing idea in Christianity.

However, 33.33 per cent of the respondents stressed on personal unity based on custom, culture, tradition and love or concern for others. The indigenous approach to unity is preferred by 22.22 per cent of the respondents, because they feel that indigenousness is the Kuki reality that can unite them. The political approach to unity is supported by 8.33 per cent of the respondents.

Who should be responsible for fostering unity?

On the question of who should be responsible for fostering unity, 5.74 per cent of the resdpondents feel that the Kuki public is mostly responsible for fostering unity, because people's participation is of paramount importance. They opined that unity is neither a new theory nor a "built in" part of a philosophical ideology but an act of *Khankho* (the Kuki way of life). Among the respondents, 25.71 per cent feel that religious leaders are responsible for fostering unity, as unity rests on self-dedication. They feel that self-willingness is the first step, which is followed up by religious leaders. Social leaders fall into the category of 11.42 per cent because they stated that they had been appointed by the society. As a social group, they are responsible for uniting the Kukis. Among the respondents , only 5.74 stated that politicians are responsible for fostering unity among the Kukis. They feel that politicians are election-minded leaders who are interested only in position and power and that their role in fostering unity can only be marginal.

What are the causes of division?

On the question of division, 31.57 per cent stated that denominationalism and church organisational chauvinism are the main causes of division. They felt that division in the name of denomination and church organisation is one of the causes of disparities in community.

Among the respondents, 28.94 per cent stated that "narrow understanding" is one of the factors of division, 23.68 per cent stated that people are not strong in faith and that faith in God can unify people groups, 13.15 per cent attributed division to clannishness and 2.63 per cent considered differences in dialect as the cause of division.

Do the respondents appreciate the coordinative function performed by All India Kuki Worship Service Coordinating Committee?

On the question of the function of AIKWSCC, 82.75 per cent of the unit leaders of KWS expressed their preference for the coordinative function performed by AIKWSCC, as they felt that AIKWSCC plays an effective role in guiding KWS to foster unity. They opined that AIKWSCC is facilitating the ministry of KWS and acts as a unifying platform for sharing of ideas. A leader has written that even though the units are independent, the relationships that exist among them make them interdependent on one another and binds them together in worship of God and service of community.

Among the leaders, 17.24 per cent do not appreciate the role played by AIKWSCC because of the denominationalism it has wittingly or unwittingly promoted. They suspect that the authority of AIKWSCC and the function performed by it may lead KWS to an institutionalised form of denomination.

What does **Pathien-Oi** *mean to the respondents?*

On the question of *Pathien-Oi*, 44 per cent of the respondents stated that they understood and agreed with the term *Pathien-Oi*. The respondents stated that it is a matter of total adherence to the will of *Pathien* and the term used to convey the idea of God. *Pathien-Oi* relates the Christian faith of God seen in Christ Jesus without any formula but faith alone. The respondents stated that it is all about following God's commandment as *Pathien* and accepting salvation in Christ.

Among the respondents, 20 per cent trust and believe in the work of the spirit as *Pathien Oi*, as they feel that God is seen in the work of the spirit; God as spirit is also stated by Jesus. They also stated that one believes in *Pathien Oi* and that this belief calls for trust in the nurturing power of the spirit of God at the individual and corporate levels.

To accept the ultimate reality of the existence of God was chosen by 20 per cent of the respondents. They stated that the belief in the existence of God is a reality presence. Another 20 per cent of the respondents had individual ideas, that is, ideas in accordance with their perception of reality.

What does "Houkhawm" mean to the respondents?

On the question of *Houkhawm*, 57.57 per cent of the respondents stated that togetherness of people in worship is *houkhawm* as coming together to worship in service is to do the will of God as a community. They asserted that *houkhawm* is a call to assemble in the faith community of God as one community people. It gathers people together in Christ.

Also, 33.33 per cent of the respondents considered *houkhawm* as people coming together to praise and pray. They pointed out that *houkhawm* is *koinonia* in the context of the Kuki people because of the communion or fellowship made possible in the gospel of Christ, where the Spirit works (1 Cor 1:9; 2 Cor 13:13; Phil 1:5). However, 9.09 per cent of the people were seen sharing their ideas of individual interest.

KWS Members' Response to the Questions of Unity

What does unity mean to you?

On the question of unity among the members of KWS, 44.92 per cent of the respondents believed that unity means coming together in agreement. They stated that unity is seen in the act of togetherness, united by being of the same opinion. They stated that unity is the outcome of agreement among the people. They further affirmed that joining people together by force cannot be regarded as unity.

Also, 40.57 per cent of the respondents chose unity as it fostered relationships for equality through fraternity and solidarity. They further stated that healthy relationships form the base of unity. In addition, 14.49 per cent of the respondents considered unity as love and healthy relationships.

For the establishment of unity, 61.29 per cent of KWS members stated that self-sacrificial love is needed for the establishment of unity. Respondents opined that without self-sacrificial love, unity could not be postulated. They also pointed out that sacrificial love is a free-will contribution and not a charity show; it is a true act of love expressed in the form of concern and care. Also, 24.19 per cent of the respondents considered religious tolerance as a prerequisite for unity and 14.50 per cent considered sensitiveness to differences as an essential prerequisite for unity.

What role does KWS play for unity?

On the question of the role of KWS, 61.01 per cent of the respondents agreed that KWS should work for unity by building relationships. The respondents stated that church organisational differences in the name of denomination, doctrine and even social wills abet separation. This instrument of organised leadership has different plans and motives. The respondents added that KWS can function as a role model for unity. It can build relationships among people in Christ.

Among the respondents, 28.82 per cent considered KWS as a role model for unity. Personal views showed that 10.16 per cent of the respondents did not know how KWS worked for establishing and strengthening unity.

What could be the foundation of unity?
On the question of the foundation of unity, 70.66 per cent of the responsdents considered Christ as the foundation of unity. The respondents stated that following Christ amounts to nurturing the community. Mending broken relationships is our duty to God. Following Christ's self-sacrificial act of love and concern is the foundation of unity.

Also, 24 per cent of the respondents considered custom, culture and tradition as foundation of unity. Among the respondents, 2.66 per cent considered the Constitution as foundation of unity. In addition, 2.66 per cent of the respondents considered mutual understanding as a prerequisite for unity.

Questions of Transformation

What does transformation mean to you?
On the question of the meaning of transformation, 57.89 per cent were of the view that ideological change for progress can transform the Kukis. The respondents felt that ideological motivation can bring transformation to personal and corporate life lore. They defined motivation as a psychological feature that arouses an organism to work for the fulfilment of a desired goal. It gives purpose and direction to behaviour. Motivation is needed to ignite a person's inner consciousness to work for social transformation. Ideology pertains to or is a characteristic of the orientation that characterises the thinking of a group or nation. They asserted that ideological motivation in the knowledge of God is required for the transformation of the Kuki community.

Also, 35.0 per cent of the respondents opined that transformation began in the mind and thinking power of the spirit that works within people. According to 7.01 per cent of the respondents, transformation means complete inner change.

How should KWS work for transformation?

On this question, 42.30 per cent of the respondents were of the opinion that KWS should act as a role model for transformation. The respondents stated that KWS, being a role model in the sphere of social, political and religious life, can bring about transformation in the people and their environment.

Also, 34.61 per cent of the respondents agreed with KWS as an agent of change for transformation. They expressed that it acts as an agent of change in the process of continuing Jesus' divine ministry entrusted to his followers by the power of the Spirit. And 7.69 per cent of the respondents were aware of the role played by KWS in transformation through participation in dealing with issues faced by the people. Personal ideas indicate that 15.38 per cent of the respondents felt that division in the name of denomination needs to be discouraged by disseminating constructive ideas.

KWS Leaders' Response on Questions of Transformation

How should all the units of KWS take part in the process of unity and transformation?

According to Table 5 (a), 59.25 per cent of the respondents agreed that KWS should take the responsibilities for fostering unity and transformation. They stated that all units need to actively participate in community life and work for the welfare of the people.

Also, 40.74 per cent of the respondents stated that the units of KWS need to participate in the process of unity and transformation by contributing ideas through coordination. They also stated that constructive ideology and plans are always in need of unity and transformation.

How to promote KWS as an agent of transformation?

In order to promote KWS as an agent of transformation, 48.64 per cent of the respondents stated that KWS can be promoted as an agent of transformation by promoting sense of oneness in the Kuki community. They stated that the mission of KWS is to find common ideologies and views among the Kukis in order to bring about transformational change. They also stated that transformation comes from spirituality, according to the scripture.

Among the respondents, 24.32 per cent stated that equal rights can promote KWS as an agent of transformation. The respondents expressed their desire to work for the welfare of the community. They stated that the Kukis need to be liberated from ideological influx of outsiders. Also, 21.62 per cent of the respondents considered KWS as an agent of change, justice and equality. They stated that KWS is community worship of *Chung Pathien*. Also, 5.40 per cent of the respondents stated that the Kukis belonged to one Lord, one faith and one baptism.

What could be the reason for growth and progress of KWS since its inception?

On the question of growth and progress of KWS, 51.61 per cent of the respondents stated that committed leaders have been the source of growth and progress of KWS since its inception. They also stated that the beginning of KWS was modest. It was the initiation of student leaders or parents through cottage meetings. They further stated that KWS leadership, at the initial stage, was voluntary out of the concern in the love of God for community. Leading duties were entrusted upon self-willed persons in Christ. Many respondents opined that the committed leadership with the traditionally known *tomngaihna* spirit in Christ is the main reason for the growth of KWS.

Among the respondents, 37.09 per cent considered inter-denominational fellowship as the reason for the growth and progress of KWS. Other reasons were given by 6.45 per cent and 4.83 per cent attributed it to non-denominational fellowship in neutrality.

What should be the immediate action for transformation?
On the question of immediate action for transformation, 48.27 per cent of the respondents stated that harmonious relationships among all the units of existing KWS can bring about immediate transformation. They expressed the view that unit leaders can play a vital role in uniting the different units.

Among the respondents, 31.03 per cent agreed that they must conduct annual consultative seminars as a step towards immediate action for transformation. They expressed that AIKWSCC should felicitate the ministry of KWS and establish harmonious relationships among the existing units. The respondents focused on the value of relationship in Christ to strengthen the nature and function of KWS. Also, 20.68 per cent of them considered enlightening the people about the gospel as the foremost priority.

Discovery Out of Empirical Research

Findings of Empirical Research for Unity
The findings of the empirical research show that unity is a form of joining together with ambition to establish relationships for equality. Denominationalism and Church organisational chauvinism play a divisive role in the community. KWS has been playing an important role in unifying and transforming the Kuki diaspora. Religious tolerance has been an approach to Kuki unity. Self-sacrificial love has always been the most ministrant prerequisite for unity. Universality of Christ, his moral code and ethical teachings can foster unity in the Kuki traditional way of life as seen in *Khankho,* custom, culture, love and concern.

Inclusive leadership, not parochial exclusive leadership, is the approach to Kuki unity. Every member is obliged to do good work with the spirit of universal tolerance by accepting one another with the same code of conduct. Members and leaders of the KWS community fellowship can participate by taking responsibilities. They should trust each other with universal tolerance in their faith in God. Motivation through conference, seminars, revival meetings, exchange of ideas and the like may promote unity. *Pathien Oi* means "God in us" and we live in God individually and corporately as our spirituality. The community nature of togetherness of people in worship in the form of get-together is known as *Houkhawm*.

Findings of Empirical Research for Transformation

Committed leaders of various units have played major roles in the growth and progress of KWS. Relationships among all the units may have an immediate impact on transformation through contribution of ideas in a coordinative way. Participation of every unit, thereby taking responsibilities, may foster transformational change. KWS as an agent of change may be promoted with relevance to unity and transformation. Love and concern are the best qualities that act as an agent of change. Seminars, workshops and crusades can function as the base for transformation of personal and social life. Emphasis on the spiritual needs of individuals and airing their grievances amidst the negativism that hinders changes through counselling can nurture our way of life. Society is always the outcome of individual spirituality. Therefore, our spirituality in Christ and educational growth can determine the way to transformation.

Summary

Division among the Kukis prevails due to the presence of multi-dialect, narrow understanding, clannishness, denominationalism and church-organisation chauvinism. Though the units of KWS have been functioning independently, the public mass has been supporting leaders with abiding love and concern as a community. KWS is airing the message of commonality, of being one group. KWS helps the people to get together in Christ for the salvation of the Kukis. It helps them to forsake their differences in the name of denomination, doctrine and church organisation. It also helps them to realise the value of humanity with special reference to the Kuki community. Clannishness, which functions as itches that disturb unity among the people, will diminish in its evilness. The inner quality of every person needs to be considered.

Love of God in Christ Jesus can foster unity for human growth. The respondents stated that the Kukis living in cities need psychological, mental and social awareness to keep the community alive. So KWS is bringing them together in the spirit of worship. They are happy to use their God-gifted dialect of scriptures as a tool for worship and for rendering service in the love of God to the community. *Khankho* is teaching the people how to respect elders and give due importance to human personality. It also teaches them how to attend to the demand of a situation with the spirit of *tomngaihna* (self-willingness). They opined that understanding the value and nature of interdependency as a community people strengthens unity with responsibility. The units of KWS function independently and yet they are interdependent. Therefore, KWS must play a crucial role in unifying and transforming the Kuki diaspora.

CHAPTER FOUR

Theology of the Kukis for Unity and Transformation

Introduction

The theology of the Kukis (Theology of Kuki Humanity) is a study of the work of God *(Chung Pathien)* in socio-cultural and historical perspective that shaped the Kukis as a human community. It is a living theology formulated in the context of life and witness of the people in terms of their struggle and aspiration in their way of life. It is a U-turn approach to Kuki self-retrospection in theology according to their way of life, nurtured by the work of the Spirit, which functions as a renaissance for unity and transformation. In other words, it can be understood as *Pathienthulogy*[1] in the culture of the Kukis. It is due to the belief of primal people in the love of *Chung Pathien*. Besides, theology is also a product of human culture in which KWS ministry is traditional and yet innovative according to the context.

---

[1] The study of God in the Kuki context is *Pathienlogy or Pathianlogy* and the study of the word of God is *Pathienthulogy/Pathianthulogy*

Why Theology of the Kukis

The need for the restoration of theology of the Kukis is a situational demand in relationship with the result of empirical study. It is to help people understand about their wilderness in socio-political and religious condition followed by economic degradation since 1917 CE. Humanity is ordained by God and nurtured in Christ Jesus, where a religion like Christianity comes after it. In the same manner, Kukis' humanity was also ordained by God in their way of life *Khankho* (theist, moral and ethical *way of life* for economy and polity), which precedes Christianity. Theology of Kuki Humanity or Theology of the Kukis existed with their belief in the existence of God for life. The Kukis can be termed as 'Theist People of God.' However, they had suffered in two ways:

- They suffered from the hegemonies of political war of freedom movements and genocide force of dehumanisation under the force of militancy in tribalism.[2] In times of enmity, law of tyranny and injustice oppressed the people and then outlaw took its place. As the result of this, the Kukis were psychologically threatened and socio-economic and political wilderness prevailed. Human values declined because of tribalism and militancy. Religion and morality became weak due to hatred and wickedness.

- They suffered because of Church organisational chauvinism. The coming of Christianity, along with the

---

[2] Haokip., *op.cit.,18 Rhetoric of Kuki nationalism*......cited that the state of the Kuki mind from 1986 to 1992 can be best described as stupefied. NSCN (IM)'s aggression was rather a surprise. More than 900 innocent Kukis were killed and more than 300 houses were uprooted in the name of Nagaland for Christ. The most horrified culture of dehumanisation in the 20th century Christians of the North Eastern India is recorded as "Kuki Tragedy" by KNO Publication 2008, *Zale'n Gam Kuki Nation.*

bags of church organisations, functions as a tool for breaking relationships among the Kukis. Christian schools of doctrine and denominations are destroying the "Unity in Community." Fragments of *Houbung Organisations*[3] functions in separatism. The spiritual pride of individualism and egoism backed by a clan-centric attitude whispered as an itch of evil sprite among people;[4] however, it is renouncing in its evilness.

KWS can help people understand their wilderness in socio-political and religious condition followed by economic degradation since 1917 CE. In order to overcome the above-mentioned hegemonies and chauvinism, KWS needs to work in the spirit of God's love seen in Christ for the Kukis. The ministry of KWS, with its focus on God and community, needs a theology that is healing and healthy in the faith of Christ's spirit at work. Faith in the will of God for the Kukis and salvation is imperative because humanity seen in Jesus Christ is life giving. It is life giving because Christ vanquished the evil force of barbaric dehumanisation of the earthly malevolent spirit in resurrection. Reconstruction of socio-political, religion and economic life depends on consciousness to meet in the already founded Kuki *way of life* called *Khankho,* with moral and ethical teachings of Jesus. Thus, the theology of humanity for people is nurturing in the Kuki way of life.

Spirit for Restoration of the Kukis

KWS can assemble and unify people according to faith and belief in the existence of the Creator. It is because it had been

---

[3] Event in a single village, two or three different church organisations or doctrinal worship service can exist, which really function as the source of separatism and groupism.

[4] Henkhovum Haolai, *Assam Gam a Kukite Thusim* (Halflong: Mungrati Press, 2009), 61.

the centre of the Kukis' ancestral faith in God. *Chung Pathien*, "Holy father above" or "Most High reigning Father", called *Chung-maangpa*[5], is the creator and sustainer of everything.[6] As far as the origin of humans, as discovered in the Kuki primal incantation known as *themthu*,[7] is concerned, the ark of container called *doibom*[8] has confirmed to us that human beings were created by *Chung Pathien*. Primal incantation is chanted as "Maker of the *leisanpa* (red soil man) comes from above; take care of him and the descendent of *leisanpa* inhabited the entire earth."[9] The sacrificial rite of laying unbroken bones of white rooster into *doibom* is performed mainly to attain a sound mind, good health and good fortune along with abundance of food grains, wealth and livestock.[10]

---

[5] *Chung-maangpa*, which means "Above reigning Father, God" is generally expressed as *Vanchung saang pen a um kapau Pathien* and *Van a um kapa Pathen*, which means our father of above, in heaven.

[6] Haolai., *op. cit 58……Chung Pathien*. See also Chongloi., *op. cit.* 134……*Chung Pathien*.

[7] Literally *them* means *proficient* and *thu* means *word*. *Themthu* is the orally inherited traditional words of incantation, chanted to protect life. Incantation is done by a primal priest to *Chung Pathien* to prosper and to refrain from further epidemics, diseases or mishaps.

[8] *Doibom* is the priestly made small bamboo basket in which unbroken bones of rooster with words of incantation are placed; it is also known as *thimthulhunbom* (an ark container of restoration).

[9] Khuplam Milui Lenthang, Manmasi Chate (Chin-Kuki-Mizo) thulhun kidang masa (Imphal: Hill Tribal Council, 2005) 6. Incantation by a priest called *Thempu; Chunga hungkon dohpa, Lhemlhung leisanpa hinsem chun, Vo Kongchan hinvop chun, Leisanpa lhaolha chun, Simlei van hinsal in,*

[10] Khuplam Milui Lenthang, "Report of Seminar on Manmasi Identity" (Imphal: LB Printer, 2009). 5, cited that: LEISANPA literally means "red soil man", the first human on the earth. According to the Kuki tradition, at the time when grains begin to appear on paddy plants, the village priest erects a pillar called *doikhom* (a type of tabernacle) in the paddy field. A bunch of paddy is tied in a tiny

It may be related to the sacrificial death of Jesus with unbroken bones for restoration of humanity on earth because it also relates the way for humans to attain eternal life in the truthfulness of the "true Son of the Father" known as *Tahchapa*.[11] This can be the presence of God at work in Spirit for the humanity of the Kukis. It is a creation narrative, found as the power of the creator *(Chung Pathien)*, God's spirit, which dwelled through their own primal incantation as a human community cared by God.

Theological Affirmation of Kuki Humanity

KWS can amalgamate its people through affirmation of faith according to the Kuki primal belief in relationship with biblical teaching and their *way of life* called *Khankho*. "Theological Affirmation" is a product of it, as Messianic People of Faith in Spirit and *Khankho*. The theology of the Kukis has put forward the already established form of unity for transformation of the Kuki community. KWS can propagate *Khankho* as a way of life, as *Khankho* comprises:

---

bundle and kept aside for the ritual called *Chaang-Nungah*, which means "Rice Maiden" Near about *doikhom*, a small thatched hut, is built where the ritual is performed. The priest and three helpers mould from the soften red clay in the shape of a man, which is dressed up in human clothing; it represents *leisanpa*, the first man on earth.

In two or three days, the priest and his helpers carry *Leisanpa* to the jungle. *Leisanpa* is propped up on a small elevated surface and two white roosters are placed by it. A ritual is performed in which a priest kills one of the roosters and smears the blood upon *Leisanpa*. The sacrificial rooster is then cooked in an earthen pot and proper care is taken that none of the bones is broken and nothing is mixed with it. The meat is consumed, leaving the bone intact and the incantation of "Maker of *leisanpa*..." is recited as given above (See also footnotes page-1 of Chapter-I).

[11] *Tah-cha-pa*–a three-syllable word, i.e, *Tah=truth, Cha=child/son* and *Pa=father*, means *true son of the father, God (Pathien)*.

- Religion: Concept of *Chung Pathen*; belief in the work of spirit, *indoi*, symbol of natural phenomena

- Polity: in the role of family administration, chieftainship *Haosa*, Kuki Inpi

- Social life-lore of *Shom, Thatep, Lawm, Kut* and *Lenkhawm* community get-together.[12]

Transformation is seen as nurtured by the Christ Jesus' Spirit at work through the Gospel way of light, truth and life in *Pathien Oi.*

The theological affirmation of the Kukis states that:

- The Kuki primal concept of *Chung Pathien* (Above/ Heavenly Holy Father) "Most High" is the Creator, God (It has a parallel meaning and common concept with *Yahweh* the Most High, God of Hebrew).

- Incarnation *(vanmileipieng)* of the spirit of *Pathien* is manifested in human one "true child of the father" God called *Tahchapa Jesu,* full of truth and grace. He incarnated through the womb of God's "Most Favoured Woman" called *sahchungnungnu* the Virgin Mary *tahchanu* by obedience. (*Jesu* is the *vanmileipieng*)

- Spirituality seen in Christ Jesus is the Holy Spirit of above "Benevolent Spirit' protective, constructive and the source of life. It is supportive, liberative, loving and caring.

- This earth is the world of God called *Chung Pathien* and the sphere of the Evil One called *lhangnel* or *Satan.*

- The evil spirit of the world is "malevolent" unprotective, destructive and dehumanising. It is the source of lust, temptation, hatred and violence and is terminative.

---

[12] Haolai., *op. cit.,* 43-60

- *Pathien Oi* is spirituality and faith of the Kukis, the trust in the "living word of God' called *Pathien thuhing* and in the work of the Spirit of *Chung Pathien*.

- The Bible is the human document and the inspired word of *Chung Pathien* (God) through humans.

- Kuki humanity is founded in the *Khankho* way of life, nurtured by moral and ethical teachings of Jesus, the *tahchapa* (true—child or son—of the father, God).

- Re-reading of the Bible to establish justice, equality, peace and integrity has to be done in the context and perspective of Kuki Indigenous Messianic Human Community.

- Men and women are equally responsible for unity, transformation and prosperity.

Unity in *Khankho*

KWS, being formal and movement-oriented, can incorporate a way of life to nurture the people by maintaining the right spirit of being one with the community. It is because internal care of KWS for the people can be incorporated by using the value of *Khankho*, the traditionally known "way of life."

Literally, *Khan* means "growth" and *kho* means "village." The combination of the two syllables in *Khankho*, which means a duty that acts as a binding force in relationships for the growth of the people. KWS can incorporate the traditional Kukis way of life in its overall approach. *Khankho* is an act of obligational duty in which the socio-political, economic and religious elements of the Kuki community life are knitted together. It is the Kuki past and present and can lead to growth and prosperity. *Khankho* can help KWS to establish and strengthen relationships among the people. Social etiquette and grace, such as greeting, speaking, sharing, loving, associating in times of sorrow and happiness and participating in special community activities, can be learned from the traditionally inherited *Khankho* way of life. Even today, *Khankho* is the main code of conduct for the Kukis. It can also be understood as the presence of Jesus' teachings in the Kuki way of life. *Khankho* can be performed by KWS even today, and Christ can be made known and kept alive among the Kukis through *Khankho* – an instrument of unity and transformation.

Young people should therefore learn and practice the *Khankho* way of life. Experienced elders teach *khankhology*[13] in words and in action to nurture interpersonal relationships. KWS can transform family administration and the village polity through the *Khankho* code of conduct. The Kuki dialects are interrelated in *Eipao*,[14] which keeps the Kuki community intact in unity and transformation.

Chung Pathien is Unity

KWS can propagate the primal concept of *Chung Pathien* to strengthen the spirit of community faith to unite the children of *Pathen*. *Chung Pathien* is the term that hails God as "Above God of Heaven" for Kuki humanity and salvation. For the Kukis the centrality of *Pathien* is seen in *Tahchapa Jesu* "the true son of father God", who is the source of unity in love, concern and care.

In the literal sense, *Chung* means "above" and *Pathien* means "Holy Father." The combination of these words, *Chung Pathien*, gives the meaning "Above Father of Holiness." The

---

[13] Village elders and parents are the professors of *Khankhology*. During primal days, *Khankho* was the orally taught principle of action for personal and community growth according to the community's way of life. It was not a written commandment but act of fulfilling various duties in life.

[14] The Kuki word *Eipao* means "Our language" in English. It is an inclusive term because all the dialects spoken by the Kuki people are commonly termed as *Eipao*. (*Eilish*, which means *our English* is an Anglo-Kuki language, i.e., English+Eipao=Eilish)

word *Chung* denotes the abode of *Pathien*, which is presumably located high up in the sky. It implies the attribute of *Pathien* as the "The Most High" God of above or heaven. *Pathien* is also poetically expressed as *Chung Maang Pa/Pathien*, which means "Above reigning Father or Heavenly reigning Holy-Father." It refers to the hallowed nature of God's name, entitled as "our father in heaven, holy is your name" *(Chung Pathien)*, the supreme God of above, who reigns in its holiness and perfect uniqueness. According to the primal incantation, *Pathien* is the central focus of religiosity. *Pathien* holds a central place in the primal Kuki religion.[15] The same primal concept of *Chung Pathien* has a parallel concept in the terms "Yahweh" of Israel, People of God. The Kuki primal traditional incantation has *Leisanpa*, which literally means "Red soil man", the first human on earth in which *Pathien* is the subject, maker of the *Leisanpa*.[16] The same concept and the central focus of *Pathien* are passed on to the Kuki translation of the Bible. The primal and biblical authentic focal point of humanity is to keep the commandment of love in *Chung Pathien* for Kuki unity.

KWS needs to make people understand that "our father in heaven, holy is your name" depicts clearly the concept and meaning of *Chung Pathien*. *Pathien*[17] is the benevolent God of blessings—merciful, gracious and the source of all goodness. It is the primary source for drawing the theology of the Kukis. *Chung Pathien* is the traditionally and biblically accepted affirmation of the work of the spirit for the Kukis. *Chung Pathien* can unite the Kukis and can enable them to grow and prosper.

---

[15] Interview with B. Lalnunzira, Lecturer O.T. Bishop's College, Kolkata; July 11, 2010.

[16] See also footnotes of chapter 1; first page on *LEISANPA*

[17] *Pathien* is known to be the source of all goodness and good will. They fear the evil one.

Kuki Faith in the Work of Spirit

KWS ministry is a movement of the people in the faith of the working Spirit of Christ for humanity. According to the affirmation of the "Son of Man" true son of father called *Tahchapa Jesu* (John 4:24), God is Spirit, spirit became human being, lived as a human and works with the power of spirit.

Primal people also believe in the work of spirit. People of the Kuki Primal could distinguish the spirit of the Benevolent One from the Malevolent One. The Benevolent Spirit is related to God of above and is known as *Chung Pathien*, which is not harmful but good, loving, caring and nurturing in everything.[18] It does not require any sacrificial offering. However, it is to be noted that primal people are concerned with the appeasement of malevolent spirits, which are harmful and destructive. Malevolent evil lives in *Si/Siphung* or *sibo/nabo* (forest water, fountain, or wetland), giants stones, mountains, etc. They believe in the existence of ghosts that could be seen or remain unseen. Ghosts exist as *Tuikhum ngahte* (ghosts that guard water fountain); *gamhoise* or *gamkaose* means wild forest evil-spirit or evil-greed. So, the need to appease the "Benevolent One" was given priority in order to get freedom from its evil spirit, which can cause diseases and death. They believe in the existence of *thilha-kho*, the village of death-ghost too. They also believe in the existence of life after death in which all the dead people live together in a village known as *Mithikho*; it means the "village of the death." A person who kills strong and big animals and feasts with his people gets reward in *mithikho*. A person who takes the head of enemies is tortured on the way to *mithikho* by the "head of lady evil" called *Kulsamnu* and serves as slave in *mithikho*.[19]

---

[18] Compassionate love and grace of God are called *Pathien ngailutna bukim*

[19] Haolai., *op.cit. 58.*

KWS as a Kuki disciple of Jesus can propagate the work of the life-giving spirit for unity and transformation. It is learned that a person involved with dehumanisation has to go through torture after death. To live for humanity during one's lifetime paves the way for life after death. KWS can nurture and build humanity by the benevolent spirit of love in family and in community.

Kuki Way of Worship Service

KWS can practise and promote indigenous messianic Kuki way of worship in the spirituality of being God's blessed community. It is to uphold the cultural value of devotion to *Chung Pathien* (God) in Christ for humanity. It is a unique and liberative way of community worship in the essence of integrity for prosperity and salvation.

Public worship service is hallowed with traditional bamboo or horn trumpet called *Pengkul/sumkawn* as "Call to Worship", followed by the beating of *Dah* (Gong),[20] and *Khong/khuang* traditional inheritance can unite them. Beating of those instruments beats up the heart of people to sing praise in worship to glorify the peaceful presence of the community spirit in Christ. Using different indigenous instruments such as *selangdah, pheiphit, gosem* and *theile*[21] can help to tone up the heart in the form of the Kuki way of worship for self-realisation, unity and transformation.

If today Kuki Worship focuses on *Chung Pathien* (God in Christ) as the source of life and blessing, it can help people

---

[20] *Dah* (Gong) is a traditionally valued instrument. *Dahpi/dahcha* are gongs of different kinds; beating of of these gongs arouses the value of true spirituality as a community people.

[21] Locally made guitar called *Selangdah, gosem* and *pheiphit* are bamboo-made musical instruments, and *theile* is the flute. *Tumging gingthei khong le dah* means all kinds of musical instruments.

with personal growth and prosperity of community life. The Kuki liturgy, which is natural, traditional and relative to custom, can be the central way of worship for unity and transformation even in today's KWS. Community feasting, like in the past, can have great value and unique corporate Eucharist where *saba* (sharing of meat) is manifestation of kinship brotherhood practised for unity and transformation.

Worship of *Chung Pathien* in the Institution of *Indoi*

The Kuki worship form of liturgy central to *Chung Pathien* is found in primal incantation. Its relationship with the biblical teaching would be prudently authentic for KWS to adopt as liturgy for community worship in faith. It is the main element of liturgy and devotional prayer of incantation that can be implemented by KWS.

Even today, the chaplain or pastor can also take the role of a primal priest called *thempu* and have freedom to minister in prayer of incantation. A priest can utilise incantation to live a long life like porcine that lives till its forehead becomes slanted or like a he-goat that lives till its horn is curved. It is a prayer of desire to posses the durable and smooth "tree" called se, the valued cosmic world tree. Prayer can seek the desire to be sufficient enough. A man's desires to get a virgin damsel and to possess tools of weapons for protection can be fulfiled. Human desires to have durability or tenderness with strong reasoning power, like the structure of the fibre layers of *Khaopi*, can be fulfiled. A minister can ask God to take care of him without deformity. As a human, he or she should serve Him according to his or her desire and will be devoted according to the will of God. Prayer can be offered to ask God that the one worshiped by his ancestor should bless and take care of humans. Prayer can be offered to ask the care and concern of mother-God called *Pathienu* and blessing of the father-God called *Pathienpa* to adorn a person. Prayers can also be offered to be like *vomgui* (a kind of growing creeper) full of networking branches that connect one tree to another and the desire to deal him generously till old age like the gourd to make relationship according to the will of God.[22]

KWS can incorporate the liturgy of the Primal Kuki way of prayer to *Chung Pathen*. Through this prayer, known as *Indoi* words of incantation, KWS can ask God to take care and seek blessings to nurture life. Incantation and chanting of *doithu* (words of *doi*), which is a prayer to God, desiring to live humanly, with health and for growth, can be practised to enrich the life of the worshipping community. This prayer of incantation can seek the blessing of God. Humanity of the Kukis today can be nurtured by *Chung Pathien* through the chanting of the words of prayer and incantation.

---

[22] Chongloi., *op. cit.*,235-237. The translated primal prayer words of incantation are given above according to the written words of incantation given as follows:

Vohpi dekon nasah bang in hinsan, Kelchal kiheh nasah bang in hinsan. Chaothenpha nasah bang in hinsan, Chemjampha nasah bang in hinsan.Haijangpha nasah bang in hinsan, Sinampha nasah bang in hinsan. Kolteng nasah bang in hinsan. Ehinsan eihinsasol hih in, eihin bolsol jih in, Kumtin ju napeng'e, kumtin sa napeng'e. Kapu houvin eihinsan, kapa houvin eihinsan, Pathennun neihin san, Pathienpan neihinsan. Lhoutinnun neihinsan lhoutinpan neihinsan, Lhochongnun neihinsan lhochongpan neihinsan. Neijilnun neihinsan, neijilpan neihinsan, Eihin sasol hih in eihin bolsol hih in. Kumtin ju napeng'e, kumtin sa napeng'e, Igan le igan kisa hen, angma le keima kisa hitin. Ijile iji kisa hitin, icha le icha kisa hitin, Tumang voijin neihinsan, haibang teh in eihinsan. Muchi toh eihinsan, chivo toh eihinsan, Changsom toh eihinsan, changja toh eihinsan. Tumang voijin neihinsan, haibang teh in eihinsan, Se nun pha nasah bang in neihinsan. Thing hepha nasah bang in neihinsan, Khaopi thosom nasah bang in hinsan.. Gopi huilhung nasah bang in eihinsan,Eihin eihin sasol hih in eihin bolsol hih in. Kumtin ju napenge, kumtin sa napenge, Vomgui pha nasah bang in eihin san. Tumang voijin eihin san, haibang teh in eihinsan.

Unity in the Symbol of Natural Phenomena

Shaking of the earth as the call of God

Kuki faith and traditional understanding of shaking of the earth as the call of *Chung Pathien* (God) could have been the core intimate relationship with God. It is a traditional saying that whenever an earthquake occurs one has to say in a loud voice: *"Manmasi chate kahing hing nalai'uve!"* It means "Children of Manmasi, we are still alive."[23] This phrase is uttered immediately in response to the shaking of the earth in order to make *Chung Pathien* know (the one who shakes the earth) that its people are still alive and that God should leave them without hindering them.

In the same manner, KWS can integrate people as a response to a natural calamity. Like natural calamities, untoward incidents like assassination and massacre can be regarded as the call of God—something that could be a reason for being united and putting more efforts into social transformation. This traditional understanding of natural calamities and other untoward incidents has a unique significance for the formulation of the Kuki theology, as it establishes a relationship between *Chung Pathien* (God) and the Kukis.

Tahchapa Jesu Is *Mi'upa*

KWS can help the people understand that Christ is present in the *Tahchapa* spirit and that salvation means liberation. It can highlight the self-denying servitude of Jesus. Literally,

---

[23] Translated incantation by a traditional priest called *Thempu:* "Oh! God of the heaven and God of the earth, we are the children of Manmasi. We are alive, we are alive; we are safe and sound; sustain us well!"

Tahchapa[24] means the "true son of the father", that is, the true son of God (*Pathien*). *Tahchapa* is a noun and the subject that works as spirit in man. It tells man to be strong in truth and to go for growth and prosperity in the spirit of the living God.

Tahchapa is the Jesus of the Kukis. Christ Jesus[25] is the *Tahchapa*[26] who stimulates human spirit because God the spirit and the divine spirit of power work in every human being. The *Tahchapa*, Jesus Christ's spirit, is the living spirit that stimulates humans to struggle with courage and determination. For the Kuki people His divine human nature of ruling in spirit adorn Him as *Lal-jesu*, the "Lord-Jesus reigns", and confers on him *Lalpa*, which means "Reigning Lord." *Pakai* in terms of His leading as "Leading father" or "Leading Lord" and "Eldest or Big Brother" *Toupa*, is personal head—someone on whom a person depends upon for everything.[27]

---

[24] *Tah-cha-pa*—three-syllable words, i.e, *Tah=truth*, *Cha=child/son* and *Pa=father*, means *true child of the father, God* called *Pathen*. The meaning of the word "tahchapa" designates the truth that cannot be changed or cannot die and could withhold eternity. It is a traditionally used slogan to stimulate a person to ignite his will power of determination to overcome obstacles. *Tahchapa's* nature of unchangeable truth is eternal, everlasting, infinite and omnipresent. In the history of the world, many humans died in search of truth but the most human one, Jesus, said, "I am the Truth," (John 14:6), and his nature of overcoming death and resurrection designates him as *Tahchapa* for the Kukis. This truth about life as seen in resurrected Christ depicts that Jesus is the authentic *Tahchapa Jesu*

[25] The reign of God in Christ Jesus endorsed him as the King called *Lal* or *Lalpa*, which means "the father who reigns", and as "leading father" or *Pakai* (literally means "leading father"). So, the reign of God in Christ Jesus is connoted as *Laljesu/Lalpa* (reigning lord) *Pakaijesu* (leading lord).

[26] *Tah-cha-Pa* can also be understood as the father, son and holy-spirit of God, personified in Jesus Christ, the most human.

[27] Interview with Lian Samte, Assistant Secy. Zomi Fellowship, Kolkata, October 03, 2010. *Toupa*, etymologically *Tou*, means "big-brother" and *Pa* means "father." Toupa is traditionally known personal head upon whom we depend for everything.

KWS Can Propagate *Tahchapa-Jesu* as *Mi'upa*

Jesus was known to be the eldest of a family of seven children, and the family was poor. It is inferred that he had shouldered responsibility as the eldest son of the family quite early in his life.[28] So, *Tahchapa Jesu*, according to his birthright, coincides with the Kuki tradition that adorned him as *Toupa/Mi'upa*.[29] According to the Kuki tradition and custom, *Mi'upa* is adorned as *Haosa* to rule the village. Hereditary succession of chieftainship is strictly maintained for *mi-upa*.[30] Therefore, the Kuki traditional custom has adorned *Jesus* as *Haosa*, chief. So, *Tahchapa Jesu* is *Haosapu* for the Kukis. The stimulative spirit of *Tahchapa* constructive dedication in love and concern can be enacted in the role of *Inpipu, Nampipu* and *Kumpi-pa*[31] as a "Minister" for Kuki humanity for unity and transformation.[32]

KWS can promulgate the thought that *Tahchapa Jesus'* inborn qualities, which establish truth and grace, are being the anointed one and his obedience to *Chung Pathien*. *Tahchapa*

---

[28] Henry H. Halley, *Halley's Bible Handbook* (OM Books India, 1999), 492.

[29] According to the Kuki tradition, *Mi'upa* is a title of genealogically known eldest of the family. Jesus was the eldest-born son of his parents and the head of the Israelites—people of God. *Tahchapa Jesu* dedicative and voluntary spirit of self-sacrifice, in the obedience of doing the will of *Chung Pathien* "father in heaven" is the already adapted spirit of *tomngaina* in the Kuki way of life. *Mi'upa* "Tomngaihna" spirit of self-sacrifice is the deepest love of *Chung Pathien* seen in the act of His only son *Tahchapa Jesu*.

[30] Traditionally, *Mi-upa* is the title given to the eldest man of a family; genealogically, the eldest man of a family

[31] Head of the Kuki Inpi (Kuki traditional House of Administration) is entitled *Inpipu* and the executive leader of the Kuki people is known by the traditionally adorned title *Nampipu*. The head of the land or empire is called *Kumpipa*, the emperor of the empire called *Kumpi*.

[32] *Humanistry* is a combination of two words: *human* and *ministry* (human+ministry).

shines as the light of the world; he is the good shepherd; he himself is the way, truth and life. He is the living bread from "Above holy-Father" *(Chung Pathien)*; he is the true vine. *Tahchapa Jesu* is death and resurrection. He was the pre-existed one and the one who said, *"I am Who I am"*[33] The *Khankho* way of life is the traditionally present *Tahchapa* Jesus' moral and ethical teaching for the Kukis. *Tahchapa* lives in the form of spirit to stimulate and nurture their knowledge, wisdom and understanding. Spirituality of the *Tahchapa Jesu* in human person can function as the source of power and strength for unity and transformation.

Tahchapa-Jesu: Tawmngaina, Spirit of Corrective Concern

The word *tawmngaina*[34] means 'self-willingness.' It is the spirit of one's inner self-willingness or dedication to fulfil the *khankho* way of life. The strong spirit of commitment to render service is expressed as *'tawmngaitah in pan lan.'* The spirit of *tawmngaina* as seen in the *Tahchapa-Jesu* is self-willingness to do the will of father God by fulfilling the mission redemption. The salvific mission in Jesus is the corrective concern of salvation for humankind.

---

[33] John 8:12, 10:14, 15:11, 14:16. 15:1, 8:23, 11;25, 13:19; Exodus 3:13; Isaiah 14:10.

[34] Etymologically, *tawm* means "strong commitment" and *ngai/ngaih* means "adherence with concern." Tawm-ngaina/ngaihna means strong personal commitment of adherence (self-willingness). In simple words, *tawmngaina* is a traditional act of self-willingness, voluntary service of the philanthropic slogan. It is also expressed in terms of, *puontho=* dutiful, *jienngai=* utile/useful *or gengi* =creditworthy. *Tawmngaina* is the "trust" of self-willingness voluntary service for humanistry as cited by *puluite/piluite..* It is found to be the innermost commanding heart of love and concern, having a parallel meaning with the spirit of *tahchapa-Jesu tawmngaina* spirit of corrective concern.

The *tawmngaina* spirit of the true son of God, *Tahchapa-Jesu*, can be expressed in terms of 'corrective concern.' To correct the evil character of humans was the main mission of *Tahchapa*. He corrected and rectified the not-good nature or image of humans. His corrective concern for humankind was manifested among the needy. His *tawmngaina* spirit of corrective concern, which served the needy, was his teaching, his service in miracles by turning water into wine, making the blind see, lamb walk and the deaf hear, feeding the multitude with a few loaves of bread and some fish, giving life to the dead, his nature of '*tawmngaina*' (self-willingness) to suffer till death for salvation, etc. From the death tomb of darkness, he himself was also rectified with corrective concern in resurrection by the spirit and truth.

Therefore, KWS as a community of *houkhawm* people needs to incorporate the *Tahchapa-Jesu tawmngaina* Spirit of corrective concern. Without blaming or mocking the weakness or inability of a person, they should learn to lovingly take care of one another by means of corrective concern because no one is born perfect. Everyone needs to look at the corrective concern of the *tawmngaina* spirit of the *Tahchapa-jesu*. Weakness to stand together in the field of politics, economics and religion and to promote Kuki humanity can be handled with the practise of the *Tahchapa-jesu tawmngaina* spirit of corrective concern in love. *Tawmngaina* is the trust of self-willingness, voluntary service for humanistry. It has a meaning that runs parallel to the spirit of *tahchapa-Jesu tawmngaina*, the spirit of *corrective concern*.

Tahchanu

KWS has been designated not only by the dedicative participation of the *Tahchapa* obedience spirit of man in God, but also the *tahchanu* spirit of women. It is the base that cares and nurtures the healthy life of the Kukis for prosperity. The equal responsibility taken by men and women is the beginning of people's strength. *Tahchanu*[35] means "true daughter." It is a traditionally used slogan to stimulate a woman to ignite her determination to overcome obstacle by enduring the spirit of power in her struggle for unity and transformation. The true daughter is also known as the "highly favoured one" called *sahchungnungnu.*

KWS can propagate the thought that *Pathien* (God) first met a woman (Mary) and not a man to establish a relationship in love for the world. Mary was in fact more responsible for taking care and nurturing the *tahchapa Jesus* so that the policy of God's love for the world must be implemented. God's favourite woman became the foundation for establshing a relationship between heaven and earth. God's highly favourite woman had the quality of *Sahchungnungnu* —a highly honourable quality. Virgin Mary is *Tahchanu* because she was a divinely favoured one. She was chosen for the incarnation of God in the image of human *Tahchapa*—Jesus (Son of Man). So, a woman is "highly favoured" (*sahchungnungnu)* if she struggles with *tahchanu* as a woman. Women should be valued for playing an important role in establishing relationships for unity and transformation; for example, Mother Mary established meaningful relationships between God and humankind and between the world of humanity and salvation.

---

[35] *Tah-cha-nu (tah=true, cha=child/daughter* and *nu=mother)* means *the true daughter of mother.* Etymologically, women use this term as parallel to the use of "tahchapa." *Tahchanu* also has a divine chosen term, *sahchungnungnu,* which means *highly favoured woman* (there is no such divine incarnated person in the form of woman), righteous virgin woman in morality and in ethical life of faithfulness.

Tahchanu–Dignity of Kuki Feminism

KWS can bring to the notice of people the contribution made by women towards growth and prosperity. In olden days, the women folk jokingly referred to themselves as *Numei Phungmang*, which means "woman losing clan." Traditionally, Kuki women do not retain their clan name, called *pu pa min*,[36] after marriage because they have to take the clan name of their husband. This is considered as two lives of women: (1) from childhood until marriage (she holds her father's clan name), and (2) after marriage (she begins to adapt herself to the family of her husband). The Kuki woman's ability to accept and adapt—to dissolve like salt in water—enables her to establish harmonious relationships. This is why women have become the main source of forming good relationships in society. The paternal family of a married woman is traditionally and customarily honoured with the title *Pute*, and her new family with her husband becomes *Tute* to the *Pute*.[37] A relationship as

---

[36] *Pu min/Pa min* is ancestral name. The clan name is the name of a forefather or clan man, not a woman's name. However, it is written as the second name denoting patriarch tradition/culture in which women are possessed by patriarch spirit, but the dignity of Kuki women lies in their femininity of tahchanu spirit and character of having the sacrificial nature of dissolving in her married family for life.

[37] *Pute* (pronounced as *poote*) is maternal uncle's family and *Tute* (pronounced as *toote*) is the family of the married daughter and her family. The title *Pute* is given to maternal uncle's family circle called *songgao* and *Tute* to her husband and children. It is the most honourable title because it makes relationship in love forgetting their differences in clans with understanding that breeding order does not unify humans. *Pute* and *Tute* relationship functions as family administration and the like. Women are the foundation of relationship between man and man, clans and clans, village and village and one place and other places for the growth of the Kuki community. Every bachelor seeks the favours of his beloved damsel *tahchanu* to make a new family.

pute or *tute* is a traditionally inborn quality of love and concern. The continuous practise of such a relationship gives equal importance to both men and women.

There is a saying about women with self-esteem: *"Tahchanu! tia itai kikikhi gah a, tawmngaih tah a kipang ahi."* It means, "We take the slogan *True-Daughter* and tighten our abdomen belt with self-determination and self-willingness to work." *Tahchanu* is Kuki feminism and "dignity" as *tahchanu* is women's slogan. As understood and practised, *tahchanu* is considered as the spirit of courage and self-determination of women struggling for growth and progress. KWS should also help women to ignite the spirit of self-esteem and self-determination among them so that they could have the freedom to hold responsibilities in order to contribute towards growth and prosperity. KWS today needs to move forward to overcome all obstacles for growth and transformation. It should play a leading role in building up a community in which women grow without fear—a community in which they have personal liberty and community freedom (Ruth 1:15-17).

KWS should promote gender equality; *Tahchanu* is equal to the use of *Tahchapa*, which shows gender equality in terms of responsibility in family and community. The word *tahchapa/ tahchanu* is not a mere slogan because, when uttered, it has the power and igniting spirit of stimulation, in which a person gets courage and strength. Therefore, the *Tahchapa/tahchanu* spirituality in Christ could be employed to unite and transform the people for growth and prosperity.

Christ for *Pathien Oi*

KWS can make people understand the nature of the *Pathien Oi* spirituality and religiosity in the *lenkhawm* (get-together) context of the people fellowship in Christ. It is because schools of different denominations and doctrines have been functioning as a sprite of division among the people. *Pathien Oi*[38] is the spirituality and religiosity of adherence to the faith in existence

---

[38] Literally, *Pathien Oi* is a combination of two words: *Pathien* means *Holy Father* and *Oi* means *trust, believe* or *accept. Oi+lou=Oilou* means "not acceptable"; it is an antonym for *Oi*. In poetic terms, *Oi* means to be *in-tone* or *to sing* of the song called *Zaila-oi*. A person sings or humps when he or she is cool, calm and collected. A chaotic or troubled mind does not have the spirit for singing.

In an interview, Hemkhochon Chongloi said that *Pathien Oi* is the primal worship of *Chung Pathien* (heavenly God) with faith and trust through the institution of *indoi*. Chungthang Thiek defined that to adhere totally to the word of God is *Pathien Oi* and it means to summit to the will of God in totality. Pu. T. Lunkim opined that spirituality that relates to the Christian faith of God as seen in Christ Jesus without any formula but faith alone is *Pathien Oi*. S. Prim Vaiphei defined *Pathien Oi* as acceptance of the work of God in the Gospel message of salvation in Christ Jesus. Lian Samte stated that following God's commandment as *Pathien* and accepting salvation in Christ enable us to become *Pathien Oi*. Pu. Lunkhoseh Singsit said that *Pathien Oi* is a belief in God's saving grace with love and obedience in His good will and acceptance of Gospel by being born again. The primal priestly way of worship was incantation of individual priest headship; however, here *Pathien Oi*, People of God, are meeting in a fellowship as worshipping community by faith, trust and obedience. A sense of unity in worship existed. B. Lalnunzira stated that faith and obedience to the words and will of God is *Pathien Oi* (Pathian-thu-awih); it refers to faith and belief in the words of God. It means converted into locally known *Pathien Oi*, religiosity of people who worship God, manifested in Christ; (*Pathian-thu-awih*, literally, it means to accept/trust in the words of *Pathian*; it is a Lushai Kuki dialect called Mizo). *Pathen-thulogy* is the study of the word about *Pathien* in *Eilish*.

Father Peter Haokip has written that *Pathien-Oi* is one in which or in whom *Pathien* is pleased or accepts, like basking in the sunshine or warmth of God. So, *Pathien Oi* means those who worship God or People of God in faith. Also, *Pathien-Oi* people are those who accept Jesus Christ as the only mediator between God the Father and themselves, while the so-called *Doihou/doichoi* (the one worship God in *doi*) asks the various spirits as intermediaries between Pathien and human beings. *Doihou/doichoi* people are not really *doihou*, but they placate the spirits.

of *Chung Pathien* (God) and to summit it to the will of God in totality. *Pathien Oi* is the belief and trust in the working of the spirit of God in humans. Life-supporting resources, such as land, forest, water, air, flora and fauna, are gifts from God. The spirituality and humanity stated in Jesus' moral and ethical teachings nurture the *Khankho* way of life.

KWS can propagate *Pathien Oi* among its people. Therefore, those who accept and trust the way, truth and life in the spirit of Christ, the *tahchapa Jesu*, are the converted *Pathien Oi*, "People of Faith." Jesus' moral and ethical teachings point towards the adoption of the *Khankho* way of life.

Some of the early characteristic norms of *Pathien Oi* are:

- To trust the love of *Chung Pathien* as stated in the Gospel of Christ and to work in the name of Jesus.

- To follow whatever the missionary people consider as mandatory.

- Strict observance of Sunday as *Pathien-ni* (Day of God), as holy to worship *Pathien*.

- The *Pathien Oi* should not eat sacrificial food, which is known as *doisa*.[39]

Primal village people talk about the people of fellowship as follows: *"Pathien ka Oi ye atiuvin akikhawm uvin, atao uvin la asa khawm'uve."* It means they gather, pray, sing together and call themselves *Pathien Oi*.

The term *Christian* was pronounced as *Kisitan* or *Khisitan* by primal Kuki people. Besides, for many primal village people converting to Christianity means submitting to the enemy because it is a threat to their traditional way of life. Besides, the British were politically arrogant and oppressive; so hatred prevailed.

[39] *Doisa* is meat offered for well-being; in which Christian faith of western missionaries considered traditional practice of religiosity as sin.

- They should abstain from drinking anything related to *zu*.[40]

- They should change their traditional way of life, such as cutting hair, changing dress, destroying materials used for traditional religious rites.

- They should stop appeasement of *sibo/nabo* (jungle wetland), also known as *siphung* (water fountain), believed to be the abode of malevolent spirits.[41]

The characters of *Pathien Oi* have a similar role with *Ekklesia*,[42] where the cross is a symbol of transformation—that which changes way of life.[43] So, KWS can unite people as Kuki disciples of Jesus for unity and transformation through trust and believe in the work of the spirit as *Pathien Oi*. It is the true source of humanity and salvation.

Some of the noted early *Pathien Oi*, People of God, "Kuki Disciples of the Gospel of Christ," are as follows:

- Thiaichongngola Thianglai from the Biate family of Saipum village, Assam, 1890.

- Ngulhao Thomsong from Thadou family of Nagaland, 1908. He was responsible for founding a church at Tujangvaichong Manipur in 1916.

- Teba Karong and Pu Longkhobel Karong from Kom family of Makokching village, Manipur, 1910.

---

[40] *Zu is* locally-made "rice beer" considered to be not good.

[41] Interview with B. Lalnunzira, Lecturer, O.T. Bishop's College, Kolkata (From Aizawl), July 11, 2010, and Hawlngam Haokip, a leader of KBC, Manipur, June 10, 2009.

[42] The New Testament word *ekklesia* means *call out to assemble as believers* in the form of *fellowship* get-together in worship as cited by Rev. Dino L Touthang.

[43] Interview with Thangsat Kipgen, General Secy. KBC, Manipur; June 16, 2010.

- Thangkai and Pu Lungpau were the first born-again persons of southern Manipur; they accepted Christ in early 1910.

- H. K. Dohnuna from the Hmar family, son of Sûnga (Chhûnga chief of Khawbung, near Champhai), Mizoram, 1914.

Unity in *Kut, Lawm, Shom* and *Lenkhawm*

KWS can initiate the process of unification and transformation through the traditional way of customs and cultural values. *Kut* is originally a community festival of the Kukis. It is a day of thanksgiving for the harvesting of grain, rice and other products of Jhum cultivation. *Kut* is a glory day of merrymaking in peace and celebration of being alive with abundant love of *Chung Pathien* in life. *Mim Kut, Chaang Kut, Lholhun Kut, Chavang Kut, Lhaambuh Kut* and the like are also observed. *Chapchar Kut* is a state festival. *Tharfavang Kut* and *Pawl Kut* are the other known Kut festivals.[44] Jesus manifests and performs his duties of sacraments, such as turning water into wine on the day of marriage and the last supper in the Passover fest *(Kalchuh Kut)*, in the context of his Jewish culture and tradition. The birth of *Tahchapa Jesu* is celebrated at *Khristakut*.[45] The spirit of Kut nurtured by the love of God for humans is a source of transformation of the Kuki community.

KWS can incorporate the teamwork seen at *Lawm, Shom* and *Kut*—the teamwork that goes with merrymaking and feasting—in its approach to growth and transformation. *Shom*

---

[44] Haokip., *op. cit.,* 15.

[45] As a matter of fact, on the origin of *Kukite Kut*, it is a proposal of Haojakhup Kipgen, Chairman, KWS-Kolkata. (The authentic Kuki term *Khristakut* is *Christakut* and *Christkut* in Eilish)

is a dormitory of learning for bachelors and celebration of youthful days. *Lenkhawm* is a get-together forum for sharing ideas. It is a get-together meant for cherishing the value of being alive as a community during days of sorrow and of happiness.

Selnit and *Sahnit*: Days of Bereavement

Ever since its inception, KWS has been keeping the tradition of condolence through obituary alive. It is one of the most honourable ways of expressing concern and respect for a human being. Loss of human life is traditionally considered to be the grimmest day of veneration. So, it is customary for living humans to observe a special day of obituary in honour of the deceased. This bereavement day is known in the Kuki community as *thipuldouni*. The day after the burial day is observed as *Thipuldouni*. Observance of such special days strengthens the communitarian life of the people. The bereavement day is observed in two ways, which are locally known as *Selnit* and *Sahnit*.

1. *Selnit* is bereavement day observed for the *thipha*; it means "good death or benevolent death." Death due to old age is considered "good death." Death due to sickness or illness is also considered good death. To mourn the death of a *thipha* person, a day of bereavement is traditionally kept as *Selnit*.

2. *Sahnit* is bereavement day observed for the *thise*; it means "malevolent death" or "gruesome death." Unexpected death due to a natural calamity, massacre, or assassination is considered "malevolent death." To mourn the death of a *thise* person, a day of bereavement is traditionally kept as *Sahnit*.[46]

---

[46] T. Lunkim, "Kukite Sahnit Nikho" (September 8, 2009); personal letter to the author.

KWS can also support the idea of honouring humanity in Jesus. It may be mentioned that the manner in which Jesus' death was honoured by His disciples is similar to the way *Sahnit* is observed.

Thatep

KWS can contribute labour, which is traditionally known as *thatep*. *Thatep* involves people working together in Christ for the betterment of community. It is a verb consisting of two syllables: *Tha* means "power" and *tep* means "appeal." *Thatep* is a call for or an appeal to render labour. *Thatep* promotes interdependence among the Kukis.

Originally, village people survived without the use of money. They depended on the human power of helping one another. The need for "hired labour" arose when the individual was unable to do the task alone. *Thatepna*[47] is done mainly to build a house and to work in a Jhum field. A summon to people for village community service is called *khotha* (village labour) or for the *haosa* (chief). Hiring labour is called *thalo* and the repayment of hired labour with labour itself is called *thasah*. The customary practice of "special appeal of help in labour" that does not need to be quittance is hosted with a "customary feast" known as *thavah* (feast of charity).[48] This tradition of *thatepna* is one of the acts to fulfil *the Khankho* way of life. Those who fulfil *Khankho* are in the spirit of *Tomngaihna*. The spirit of *Tomngaihna* is the inner commanding force of self-willingness that stimulates a person to render service to uplift him or her

---

[47] When suffixed, the verb *Thatep* with a single word "na" forms the noun word *Thatepna*. It is a Kuki traditional custom of appeal to work together by contributing money, wealth, wisdom, knowledge and strength.

[48] H. S.Yampao, "Thatepna" (January 20, 2009); personal mail to the author.

and neighbours and society as well.[49] The work of God in Jesus is still appealing for unification of the Kuki people in their way of life through the commandment of love in Christ and through the blessed interconnected dialects.

KWS can advocate use of *Thatep* for remodeling the temple of God called *Pathien Hou-in* in the form of "Tower of *Houzilja*." It is because *thatep* is not only the Kuki way of life and custom, but also a tradition of Jesus. With this act of appeal *thatep*, the most human one and the divine incarnate word of God, *Tahchapa Jesu* called out his twelve disciples. They followed him to minister humankind according to the will of God for humanity and salvation. Like the act of *thatep*, the present Kuki community can also practice the tradition of love and concern for unity and transformation.

Unity in the Body of Animal

KWS can suggest that meat could be eaten at *Khrista-Kut* and other festivals by the worship community as it has Eucharistic value. *Sa* means animal. Among the animals *sel* (mithun/bison) is one of the traditionally most valued animal. Meat has cultural and traditional value in Kuki family administration. The body of the animal that has been killed is divided among the family members. This tradition of sharing is meant for recognising "who is who" in the family according to the *Khankho*. *Sating* (the backbone of an animal) is given to the eldest brother or big brother called *mi'upa/toupa* in recognition of being a "big brother." It is given to acknowledge the person as head of the family. The administration of family affairs rests on the head of the family. *Sating* symbolically means *mi'upa/toupa*—the backbone of the family in which *Lamjaangpa (Guite)* is given

---

[49] Ngamkhothang "Understanding Khankho Thatepna" posted on Kukiforum on January 27, 2009 (*Khankho chondan in, ekhanletna diuvin tha atiem jing'e*).

sating. Pu Guite performed traditional *selpangsut*[50] with genealogical inscription.[51] It is because he is genealogically known as *toupa/mi'upa* (big brother). It is a tradition to give *sating*[52] to the eldest brother in recognition of his being the

---

[50] The Kuki traditional rite *Selpangsut*; the eldest brother of a family has to pierce the side of *sel* (mithun/bison); this is termed *Selpangsut* and the eldest brother is regarded as the backbone of the family.

[51] *Genealogical inscription of Pu Songthu, the great Patriach*: We, the descendants in the royal lineage of Pu Songthu, on this day, 2nd August, in the year of the Lord two thousand and ten, hereby, inscribe on stone the genealogy of our ancestry to mark the auspicious ocassion, *sating peh*, a traditional obligation of the younger brother to perform the ritual of offering a portion of flesh on the spine of an animal to the elder brother, has been solemnly observed in order of seniority, Pu Guite of Lamjaang, the eldest in the lineage of Pu songthu, received *sating* from Pu Doungel of Aisan, eldest in the lineage of Pu Thitou. Pu Doungel of Aisan received *sating* from Pu Kipgen of Leikot, the eldest in the lineage of Pu Touhin. Pu Kipgen of Leikot received *sating* from his twin brother, Pu Haokip of Chassad and from their *pangah* (uncle), Pu Chongloi of *Jaangnoi*. Pu Kipgen of Leikot shall receive *sating* from *pangah* Pu Hangshing of Vongjaang and Pu Thadou of Jampi, his youngest brother. So, bless us God!

[52] *Sating* (the backbone portion of animal; the traditional symbol of honour): Aisan Inpi Sunga Sating Chedan Suhtohna, *documentary film* (Kholmun: August 2, 2010) shows. Pu *GUITE* being recognised and acknowledged as the big brother (*toupa/mi'upa*) according to ancestral family genealogical tree of the Kuki people from the descendents of *Chongthu*. Lamjaangpa *(Guite)* received *sating* from Aisanpa (Doungel). Then Aisanpa (Head of Pu Doungel) received *sating* from Leikotpa (Head of Pu Kipgen) and Leikotpa (Kipgen) received *sating* from Chahsatpa (Head of Pu Haokip).

Chassadpa (haokip) gives *sating* to *Leikotpa* (kipgen) in recognition and honours him as *mi'upa (haokipgen-inpi); Leikotpa* (kipgen) then gives sating to Doungel (Aisanpa) and Aisanpa (Doungel) gives *sating* to Lamjaangpa *Guite*. It is one of the examples to show regard and honour, in which others can also practise.

It is the quest of the thesis whether *Pu. Guite* has lineage to give *sating* to the "true son of the father" *Tahchapa*, as "big brother" called *Toupa-Jesu* also known as *Israel Jesus* by faith and tradition. *Sakong*

eldest brother or big brother (*mi'upa/toupa*). It can be incorporated in the days of success or promotion in the field of professionalism.

Piercing the Side of Jesus and *Selpangsut*

According to the Kuki custom, the rite of piercing the side of *sel* (mithun) is traditionally done by the eldest man called *mi'upa*. The animal is killed for the ceremonial rite. Likewise, the begotten son of God was also the eldest one from God, who adorned Him as *mi'upa*. There is a close affinity between the piercing of the side of Jesus and the *Selpangsut*,[53] which is officiated by the *mi'upa* for the people. The noted similarity can be stated in Jesus, the *mi'upa*, who officiates his ministry of love, justice, peace, equality and salvation for humankind according to the will of His father God.

Distribution of Meat

For the Kukis a slaughtered animal or an animal killed in hunting or caught in a trap serves an important function than just being mere food for consumption. The meat of the animal slaughtered for *sa-ai*, *chang-ai* and *chon* is customarily distributed among relatives according to their positions in the

---

(hipbone) is given to the *Tubul/tucha* as a sign of being born of a daughter. *Sangong* (a portion of neck) is given to *Pute* as a sign of origin of mother. *Nahgupheng* awp/op (portion of rib bone) is given to the *bepa* as a sign of being the right hand for family administration. On a special occasion, *Saba* (peaces of meat containing every outer and inner part) is given to important delegates as a sign of covenant for a mission.

[53] "Aisan Inpi Sunga Sating Chedan Suhtohna", documentary film (Kholmun: August 2, 2010), shows Pu *Guite* being recognised and acknowledged as the eldest brother (*toupa/mi'upa*), head of the Songthu clan called *Bulpipa* (according to ancestral family genealogical tree of the Kuki people from the descendents of *Chongthu*) perform the rite of *selpangsut* to begin the custom of *satingse*.

kinship structure—spinal flesh is given to *u-pa*, neck to *sunggao*, head to the village chief, rib to *becha*, waist to the priest and so on. This shows the importance of the kinship relationship they have. Ceremonies and functions are incomplete without the participation of these people. The customary distribution of meat also has a wide-ranging political implication. It continues to be a customary practice—an important part of culture.[54]

KWS can also make people adopt any felicitation programme in the traditional "animal rite" called *selpangsut* or *sa'ai*. It can be applied to felicitate a person on the glory day of success or happiness. A successful person can be lauded with the "Song of Courage" called *hanla*.[55] Felicitation at the feast can include the distribution of gifts symbolising the traditional use of *saphe*, *sathin* and *salung* in the traditional form of *saba*[56] as manifestations of love and respect in *Khankho*. The purpose of the feast is to strengthen the kin circle of relationship in the rites of administration. The body of the animal symbolises the sacrificial death of Christ for the unity of humankind.

---

[54] Lhunkhosei Mate, "A Study on Sabasten Kappen's Understanding of Culture and its Relevance for Kuki Culture in Manipur" (M.Th Thesis, Senate of Serampore College, 2011)

[55] The *Song of Courage* called *Ha'nla* on the subjugation of animals, sung as follows: *Khul' a kapenni ne, Lai sa kano nin ne, Ka chun le jo'n, Lhaanglam chembang neichoiyo, huisi hunglang silsel'e, muol'a gegote nupa'n, keitha lambang nathei nah-e mo…, tah chapa! kapa chapa, katha noinung keima chung nung, li. li. li. li. ho. ho. ho. ho.* English translation: *"Born am I from* khul, *I set off for hunting, my parents has lifted me up like the sparkling sword, in the bliss of forest. Don't you know* gegote-nupa *(couple of the hills) that I am the one who subjugates. Vanquished is the killed and I am the victor.* Ends with "Lauditive Cheer" *li. li. li. li.li. li. li li. li* by leader and in reply *ho. ho. ho. ho. ho. ho. ho. ho. ho* by the gathered people."

[56] *Saba* is a bunch of meat tied together (containing inner and outer parts of animal called *sathin* (liver), *salung* (intestine) and *saphe* (flesh) to show unity in kinship according to the *Khankho* way of life.

The Kuki Polity of Chieftains' Unity

KWS can make people law-abiding citizens. It is because the civil government is ordained by God, even though it is often run by currupt men, to restrain the criminal elements of society. Communities as made by God are blessed with dialects or languages for communication. So, the polity of the Kukis is an acceptable norm that constructs the theology of humanity (Gen 11:5-9). The traditional Kuki polity is classified into three levels: Family level, village level and *nampi* or national level.[57] Chieftainship is the basic form of Kuki traditional governance in the villages, like Greek city-states.[58]

KWS can ordain the democratic system of Haosa

There cannot be *Haosa* without people. Leaders of the Kukis are traditionally known as *haosa*, leaders of the people and for the people. *Haosa* is the chief leader who lives for the security of land and people. Chieftain's unity is the reign of Kuki polity and is still the bond of unity inherited from their ancestors. In the present context, *Haosa* is the traditionally authentic title given to the appointed or elected person who cares or looks after the welfare of people in towns or cities. KWS can enact and ordain the democratic system of *haosa* administration

---

[57] See also Kuki Polity of chapter 1 for details about family and national level

[58] George T. Haokip wrote "Chieftainship of the Kukis" in *The Sangai Express*. This article was webcast on April 29, 2009. Each village has a chief called *Haosa*, the hereditary owner of ancestral lands. *Haosa/Lal* is traditionally the repositories of all powers of administration dealing with the village. His rule is autocratic but not despotic. *Haosa* is primogeniture succession. Hereditary succession of chieftainship is strictly observed. The first-born child *mi-upa* succeeded as the village chief and inherited his father's property. Kuki *Haosa* (chief) reigns with enormous power of executive, legislative, judicial and military power. He also looks after the issue of ordinances, framing of rules and regulation. The chief runs his business through the help of *upa (elders)*.

because it is the peoples' elected or selected person who looks after the affairs of the people. It is visible in the form of centralisation or decentralisation. This polity needs to be preserved by the leaders of the churches in order to strengthen and promote the spiritual and social growth of the people.

Kuki Inpi

Kuki Inpi, the traditional House of the Kuki government (parliament), is the highest court of appeal for the Kuki people. It is also known as the apex body of the Kukis. The pattern is replicated at the *Gamkai* or the state level, and *Lhaang* refers to the district level. *Haosa*, chiefs of the villages, are members of it. Traditionally, the Kukis considered the first-born male child or "big brother" called *Mi'upa/toupa* as the family administrator. His administration is known as *Upa Inpi*, in which the family issues of women and others are managed by him. But at the Nampi level, it is the head clan of the Kuki family like *Guite-Doungel Inpi*.[59]

Unity and transformation from diasporas

The Kuki diaspora can contribute a lot towards unity and transformation as it is cognizant of other cultures and traditions. Their knowledge of the value of cultural identity and Gospel identity can help them unite and transform and remodel themselves.[60] KWS can make people understand the revival of the traditional *Kuki Inpi*, which has remained latent

---

[59] The function of *Upa-Inpi*; *Guite-Doungel Inpi* is genealogically the head clans of the descendent of Chongthu. *Hmar inpui, gangte inpi, vaiphei inpi, paite inpi(pnc), chonghang-inpi, khongsai inpi, haokipgen inpi* [Chassatpa *(haokip)* give *sating* to Leikotpa *(kipgen)* in which the twin brothers recognition of the first born is traditionally honoured] is the tradition of *Khankho* way of life in honour and in the love of traditional forefather's relationship.

[60] An Interview with Father Peter Haokip Tongmang, Vice Rector, OTC, Mawlai, Shillong; May 11, 2010; 11:00AM.

since India gained Independence. It was revived due to the crises faced by the Kukis from the 1980s and the 1990s.[61] So, the polity of the *Kuki Inpi* functions for the unity and transformation of the people to establish justice, equality and peace.

Traditional Use of Weapons Among the Kukis

In the remote past, the Kukis used weapons for hunting animals for food or for self-protection. Bows and arrows (*thal or thalpi*) were used for hunting animals and big birds. They also used a weapon called *Gophel*, which is made of bamboo, for hitting objects. A small catapult-like weapon (rubber-made *gophel*) was used for shooting birds and small animals. They also invented a gun called *meipum* or *pummei*. It is also known as *Thihnaang* or *thihnaanglong*, as it has a long hole in it, where gunpowder is put and used. A weapon called *pumpi* was invented during the initial days of the British Raj.

They made guns to protect themselves against the evil force of barbaric dehumanisation. Guns were not meant to be pointed at human beings, which is traditionally expressed as *thal a mi kidoi ngailou ahi*. It means "do not point a gun at a human being." Mad or evil men misuse weapons, but a sane person uses them to hunt animals for food and to protect human life. The care and concern for life is evident in a saying like *mihiem lamlhahna lang nga in thal muh akikoi ngaipoi*. It means "a gun must not be pointed at the way of human."[62] Weapons should be used for

---

[61] See also *http://www.kukination.net/history.php*

[62] Recollection of the authors' childhood memory, discourse with his relative grandfather *Pu Demkhotong Haokip* of Aishi village way back in 1987. *Pu Demkhotong (Patong)* was a well-known animal hunter of his village. The author was taught with the help of simple words of quotation while he played around his grandfather. On such occasions, his grandfather usually oiled and exposed his gun called *thihnaanglong* in the sunshine of his house called *leituol*.

hunting animals for food and it is also use for the protection of *gam-le-nam*. They should contribute towards celebration of life and protection of Kuki humanity.

Naming System (*minput*)

Naming is an important practice. Jesus summoned Lazarus by his name (John 11:43) when his body lay in his grave. In the Kuki society, the naming system occupies an important place. In the process of naming a person, each syllable should highlight the character of the person. The first syllable of a person's name is always taken from the name of the person's grandparent. Let us consider an example. Suppose a person's name is *Ngamkhoson*, and his grandfather's name is *Shemngam*. It means that his name is a continuation of the name of his grandfather. The syllable *ngam* is common to both the names. In the same manner, a woman's name starts with the first name of her grandmother. Each syllable of the name is given according to the choice of parents or grandparents.[63]

Contradiction: It is an anti-traditional and dehumanising act—factional Internal Militancy (IM) of tribalism is dehumanising its own fellow humans by procuring weapons from outsiders, weapons like *AK-47, G-3, LMG, Pistol,* etc. Outlaw militant groups professing *Christian faith* are violating Kuki Human Rights.

Press release by Geneva Call: The Kuki National Organisation (KNO) of North East India commits to the anti-personal mine ban, Geneva 9, 2006—Awareness and support of Geneva Call's action in India progress as second armed non-state actor, the KNO and its arm wings, committed today on a total ban on anti personal mines by signing, Geneva call 'Deed of Commitment' (DoC) on 9 August, in the Alabama Room, in the City Hall of Geneva. It is an honor to the traditional Kuki way of life *Khankho* because it is upholding and promoting Kukis humanity, life of neighbours and human rights as a whole.

[63] Lhunkhosei Mate, *"A Study on Sabasten Kappen's Understanding of Culture and its Relevance for Kuki Culture in Manipur"* (M.Th Thesis; Senate of Serampore College, 2011).

This system helps one to trace one's genealogical line accurately for many generations. The Kukis have a patriarchal social system that traces their genealogy to maintain their *u-pa–nao-pa* hierarchical relationship. It is also used in all-important rituals, including customary burial services. But the appearance of western names and biblical names in recent times cannot be ruled out.

Ankuong sokhawm: **Table-fellowship in** *Khankho*

The term *an* means *food, kuong* means *plate* and *sokhawm* means *taking together by hand. Ankuong sokhawm* means eating together by using and sharing a giant plate made of wood. A local giant wooden dish was traditionally used as a plate for occasional *ankuong sokhawm.* It is also called *ankuong umkhawm* meaning 'encircling the plate of food', because the gathered friends or kin circle comes together around the plate for the purpose of eating together, which is called *nehkhawm/chahkhawm.*[64] In *ankuong-sokhawm,* curry is placed in the middle, where the food encircles the curry; hands are used for eating; no spoon of bamboo or wood is used. This tradition is most appropriate for 'table fellowship' of Jesus for *Khankho* way of life.

Jesus said, "Whoever does the will of God is my brother and sister and mother." In the same manner, the Kuki *khankho* also insists on human and creation relations and sets relations right and overcomes boundaries separating individuals, ethnic tribes, nations and races. Feeling pity for captives, differently-abled persons and the needy, feeding the poor, offering drinks

---

[64] Traditionally, banana leaves play an important role when a community feast is hosted by the village people *nehkhawm/chahkhawm.* Lines of locally made planks are arranged as rows of table, upon the rows of planks, living banana leaves are use for public feasting, replacing giant wooden plates called *ankuonglien (ankuonglien* means *giant wooden plate or big plate).*

to the thirsty, pardoning a fellow human being, performing customary duties, acting according to customs, laws and traditions and all other virtues constitute the *Khankho*.[65]

Eucharist was an attempt on the part of Jesus to anticipate the form and nature of the meal of the reign of God to come. It is also Jesus' practice of restoring total wholeness of the body and soul and a foreshadowing of the wholeness of the end of time. While introducing this institution, Jesus befriended the outcastes, the sinners, the crippled, the lepers, the hungry, the miserable, the blind, the lame, the prostitutes, the tax collectors, the demoniacs, the overburdened, the downtrodden, the captives and the babes or the lost sheep of Israel. These constitute the multitudes Jesus wanted to be with. That led his enemies to accuse him of being "a glutton and a drunkard, a friend of tax-collectors and sinners!" (Matthew 11:18f NRSV). Most interestingly, most of his faithful disciples came from these categories of people: "Those who are well have no need of a physician, but those who are sick, I have come to call not the righteous but sinners" (Mark 2:17 NRSV). So, we can say that the undue solidarity extended towards this community of the socially shunned category of people is nothing less and nothing more than the Kuki traditional practice of *Khankho*.[66]

The KWS community fellowship can encourage and practise table-fellowship in *Khankho* to strengthen the bonds of love, care and friendship among the members of the Kuki community and between the members of the Kuki community and members of other communities. It preserves what is good

---

[65] Lhunkhosei Mate, *"A Study on Sabasten Kappen's Understanding of Culture and its Relevance for Kuki Culture in Manipur"* (M.Th thesis; Senate of Serampore College, 2011)

[66] *Ibid,*

in earlier forms of communal life. Everyone becomes a brother, sister, mother, or father to everyone else without exception. The table-fellowship of Jesus is solidarity shown in the shadow of the cross. It is the revelation of beauty, goodness and love anticipating the nature of the meal of the reign of God and restoring the wholeness of the body and soul, which is the foreshadowing of the end time. This solid love, pity and compassion flowing out of the table-fellowship of Jesus is *Khankho*. The reciprocal goodwill relationships that are established through *Khankho* are manifested in the various aspects of the Kuki peoples' social, economic, political, religious and ethical relations.

Hemkhaam, Salam Sat and *Toltheh*: Nurturing Kuki Humanity

The word *hem* means sword (*daos*) and the word *khaam* means to cease or stop. So, the word *hemkhaam* means to stop violent acts of dehumanisation. It upholds humanity in peace, equality, love and justice. Kuki traditional culture promotes non-violence. When a person intentionally or unintentionally kills someone, the culprit's family kills a pig in the chief's house for *hemkhaam* (like present day cease-fire) in order to avoid the victim's family revenge. The Court of Housa/Lal (Court of the village Chief) has inherited this *hemkhaam*. It is done when violence occurs to avoid further violent use of weapons in retaliation. Once the rite of *hemkhaam* has been carried out, both parties are bound by the Law of *hemkhaam* and violence has to be stopped and arbitrated through peaceful means. *Hemkhaam* acts as the source of negotiation. The murderer has to pay the following for the performance of *hemkhaam*:

- *Selpi khat* (one Mithun) for *Kosana* (burial rite)

- *Khipi chang ni* (two beads) for the eyes

- *Dahpi khat* (one gong) for his Pillow

- *Pondum khat* (one traditional shawl) for winding sheet[67]

---

[67] Satkhokai Chongloi, Unpublished Dissertation of D. Min, entitled *Culture and Traditional Unity: Context of the Church's Mission Among the Kuki People in Manipur India,* (UTS Philippines, 2003), 38-40

Case study of Hemkhaam with Meetei/meitei community: Two Kuki youths, namely *Paolenlal Chongloi* from Keithelmanbi Military Colony and *Paokhosat Kipgen* from Bongbal Kholen, who were students of NEHU, Shillong, on their way to celebrate Christmas at *Bongbal Kholen* were unfortunately lynched by Nongbrang Meitei villagers in Thoubal District, Manipur, on the fateful day of December 22, 2009. The two were mistaken for members of the Kuki militant group operating in the area. According to the Meteis version, those two students belonged to the militant group that attacked the village and rode away with a TATA-704. Contrary to their claim, the people of Bongbal kholen and Keithelmanbi Military colony claimed that the two were students of NEHU, Shillong, who came for Christmas holiday and were on their way to Bongbal Kholen to celebrate Christmas. Hill tribes' social organisations like KSO, ANSAM, ATSUM, KUMHUR and KMA blocked the NH-39 for a day and some of the Metei Leaders from UCM and AMUCO, with the help of the government of Manipur, visited the spot and the families of the victims. The Government of Manipur took the initiative, and the conflict was resolved by performing *Hemkhaam* on 31.12.2009. The Nongbram Meiteis performed *Hemkhaam* by killing a pig and admitted their crime before the Court of Bongbal Kholen Chief.

Hemkhaam with the Government of Manipur: The latest incident happened when *Manggoulen Haokip,* on the night of November 17, at National Games Village, was shot dead by unknown miscreants. To settle the tension arising out of the killing, the State Government signed a memorandum of agreement with KSO, Imphal Branch, on November 19, 2010. According to the agreement, the State Government assured that the culprits would be arrested at the earliest and the customary *Hemkhaam* would be imposed in order to avoid unwanted revengeful acts. The agreement was signed by the President of KSO, Imphal Branch, Helal Khongsai and the General Secretary Seiboi Haokip on behalf of the student body while IFC/Sports Minister N Biren Singh, TD Minister DD Thaisii, MLA of 46 Saikul A/C Doukhomang Khongsai, HAC Chairman Thangminlen Kipgen and MLA of 41-Chandel A/C Thangkholun Haokip signed on behalf of the Manipur State Government.

Salam-Sat

Salam-sat is a customary rite of reconciliation for immoral guilt and sin. The Kukis consider an adulterer or fornicator as a person of low character, and she or he becomes the object of public ridicule. A boy who commits adultery with a young unmarried girl is asked to take her as his wife. But if he refuses to marry her, he has to perform *Salam Sat*, a customary practice, and pay the girl one *Mithun* as fine for the immoral act. If the boy wants to take the girl for his wife without her consent, he will have to fulfil the strictures of customary law. If the girl is pregnant, she is asked to deliver the child and take care of it for about three years. Then the boy can pay a *Mithun* and a steel gong and take his child. If a wife commits adultery willingly, she is divorced and sent back to her parents without any payment of penalty of divorce. However, if she repents of her sins and asks for forgiveness and if her husband forgives her, she can be his wife. If a woman is raped, then the one who raped her would have to kill a pig in the House of the Chief. His *Upa* (older brother or head of his family) would be fined *sel* mithun. The *Upa* of the woman's husband would receive the *Mithun*. This is done in order to avoid the problematic game between the couple.[68]

Tuoltheh

Tuoltheh means to avoid further blood-set. A customary rite, it is performed to prevent blood-set that defiles the ground. The Kukis avoid committing murder. There is no capital punishment (killing) in the Laws of the Kukis, but *bultuh* (chained to a big log) is done as life-long punishment. A person who loses temper and tries to kill or threaten another person is penalised. He has to kill a pig in the Court of the Chief of

---

[68] Satkhokai Chongloi, *Conflict Resolution in North East India: Perspective of the Kukis (Paper presentation)*

the village and promise not to repeat the misbehavior in the future. If a person is injured and sheds blood in a fight, both of them have to appear before the Village Court judges; the parties involved should first make a settlement on the shedding of blood, as the ground is defiled when blood is spilled on it. The one who sheds blood has to kill a pig in accordance with the custom called *Tuoltheh*. As far as *tuoltheh* is concerned, when blood is shed, the village ground is defiled. When nature is defiled, God is not happy; and so nature needs to be cleaned.[69] It is clearly indicated in the incantation of the *tuoltheh* ritual:[70] Various animals are used as penalty for violating the law. So, the person is free once again and the defiled environment is cleansed.[71]

The *Tahchapa-Jesu* nature of the self-sacrificial blood of the cross, which restores humanity and salvation, may have been a manifestation symbolising the nature of *Hemkhaam, Salam Sat* and *Toltheh*, as it restores peace and harmony as a *Khankho* way of life, inherited in the name of tradition. The rite of *Hemkhaam, Salam Sat* and *Toltheh* can practiced in spirituality affairs and in the name of Christ Jesus. The life-giving spirit of *Tahchapa-Jesu* has to be the leader in taking care, nurturing and mentoring Kuki humanity in the tradition of *Hemkhaam, Salam Sat* and

---

[69] Satkhokai Chongloi, *Conflict Resolution in North East India: Perspective of the Kukis (Paper presentation)*

[70] The incantation of the *tuoltheh* ritual is as follows "......*na Vohpi maikem bohni solang, alu khonah a paiyin lang chonset kinotdoh tante; ato khotoa paiyin lang chonset kinot lha tante; Pathen thu ahi'*". (... *cut your mother pig that has a slanted forehead into two halves. Throw the upper halve towards the north of the village, which will push out sins. Throw the lower halve toward the south of the village, which will push out sins. This is the word of God*).

[71] The following incantation shows how nature is restored: "*Tunin phupi akentai phaipi akentai. Kaleiduppi hungthouvin, kaleithopi hungthouvin*" (*The evil elements have retreated today; let the fecundity of my loamy soil be restored*).

Toltheh. The KWS people of *Houkhawm* can practice the above-mentioned way of human cultural reconciliation to promote non-violence, love, peace, justice and equality among its people and among other communities and in the environment. The Village Court of the Kukis is one of the fastest courts in the world, as it does not have pending cases.

Summary

In this chapter, the theology of Kuki humanity has been suggested for the unity and transformation of the Kukis through the ministry of KWS. Inter-relative dialects and socio-cultural lineage have been an indispensable binding matrix for Kuki unity. Their preferred names and government recognition may designate the Kukis as a group or sub group, but the force that binds them together consists of their concept of Spirit as God, interconnected dialects, culture, custom and tradition.

For the Kukis, unity is the established factor of commonality in their community way of life given by God and inherited from their ancestors. Religion is included as a traditional *Khankho,* way of life. The Kuki traditional spirit of "get-together" called *Lenkhawm* is all about gathering the people in fellowship. It also refashioned students in terms of "Fresher's Meet." *Lenkhawm* still awakens and nurtures the community life lore. Success for unity does not just happen; it is built daily in prayer, humanity, devotion, sacrifice, hard work and love for one another. For the Kukis, worshiping the Creator through the spirit, which is at work in their way of life, is the base for unity.

The gospel of Jesus Christ needs to be proclaimed in word and deed. Christ is the Lord and Master who shines for humanity, growth and good of the people. KWS should promote spiritual growth, social justice and equality.

General Conclusion

The existence of Kuki Worship Service in the fellowship way of get-together hails the inner intimate spirit of commonality in the knowledge of God in worship. Participation, obedience, tolerance and sacrificial act of commitment in the spirituality of Christ for community are the pillars of KWS. It was formulated by the initiation of the lay people, i.e., parents and students, with care and concern. The KWS functions with the binding spirit of *tomngaihna* in the love of God and concern for the community. For the KWS community, humanity and salvation are the sources of love and concern.

The best part of the Kukis is the heritage of their interconnected languages or dialects and unity in culture, custom and tradition. The Kukis have to worship *Chung Pathien* in service (KWS) for humanity and salvation in accordance with their "Way of Life" or *Khankho*. It is because their Way of life is nurtured by the Bible and the Word of God works in the *Tahchapa* Spirit of Jesus and *Tahchanu* spirit of women's dignity. Tradition, custom, culture, folklore, folk tale, religion and polity are known in terms of *Khankho,* the ancestrally inherited native Kuki village way of life.

Khankho is an act or an obligational duty in which the socio-political, economic and religious life of the Kukis are knitted together in humanity. *Khankho* is Kuki past and present. It is also for future growth and prosperity. Its moral and ethical authenticity is rooted in the biblical teachings of Kuki realistic humanity in the spirit of *tomngaihna*. The reason is that it is about ordinary people, not perfect people. It is a community that needs to grow without fear, looking towards personal liberty and community freedom in the love of God. The faith that the Kukis have in *Chung Pathien* gives them hope, and the love that they experience in the knowledge of God seen in Jesus beautifies their humanity.

Houzilja: Mission Humanistry in Christ for *Gam Le Nam*

The KWS *Houkhawm* people of fellowship, with the spirit of unity in Christ, can advocate the reign of love and concern for the people. It can undertake the task of building a community centre or a temple of learning and worship with due honour to *Chung Pathien* and Christ for its people.

Let us look at the term "Houzilja." This is a three-syllable term. The syllable *hou* means worship, *zil* means learning and *ja* means honour. In all, *houzilja* means meditational or devotional worship with the rites of sacrificial offering to God and learning about how to attain wisdom, skills or knowledge in the highest respect of honour. It is an act of learning how to worship *Chung Pathien* according to Christ Jesus' act of sacrificial offering for humanistry and salvation. Therefore, *houzilja* is a temple of learning about how to do the will of God with deep adoration of devotion, rites of offering called *maichaam* or liturgies to nurture the Kuki way of life. It means to do the service of humanity by seeking the will of God in the spirituality of the divine human person called *Tahchapa-Jesu.*

The Kuki primal understanding of *zilja* has been the most appropriate temple of *Houzilja* in which Christ Jesus works for the growth of Kuki humanity. *Houzilja* imparts the knowledge of God's love for the Kukis. The basic spirituality of *Houzilja* as the temple of God is founded in the becoming of God as a human person called "Christ Jesus" for Kuki humanity and liberation or salvation. He is the centre for understanding the value of every aspect of life.

For the Kukis, the temple of *houzilja* can function like a synagogue, a Buddhist monastery, a Hindu ashram and a chapel. The focus is on learning to understand the realistic existence of God in Kuki theology and manifestation of God in the gospel of Christ Jesus. Its function of faith is in the existence of *Chung Pathien,* worship in truth and spirit and service according to the Gospel of Christ Jesus for Kuki humanity, prosperity and salvation.

The Tower of *Houzilja* or Temple of *Houzilja* is a centre for learning the value of life in the knowledge of God. It can be a temple or tower for training, meeting, confession, devotion, dedication and meditation. It is a heritage centre for learning how to nurture the Kuki way of life. The main theme of *Houzilja* is to seek and to do the will of God for Kukis humanity, growth and salvation

Mission Humanistry in Christ for *Gam le Nam*

God appeared on earth in the form of Jesus Christ. Jesus is the child of *Chung Pathien*.[72] The mission that focuses on humanistry[73] (human-ministry of God) is the mission of God. Mission belongs to God and God in Christ Jesus manifests a life-giving ministry. It is the humanistry of love, peace, justice, equality and liberty. This mission is the manifestation of God's abundant love for humans, who have been created in His own image, as humanistry and salvation from sin.

For the Mission Humanistry, the redeeming act of God in Christ Jesus is the messianic mission of humanistry for humans, particularly the Kuki humanistry. It is a wholistic mission of humanistry (human-ministry of God). Humanistry has been established by God in Jesus. It is seen in the Gospel of Christ, which focuses on love for humanity.

---

[72] *Chung* means above, which refers to the "Most High" and *Pathien* means Holy Father. Most High God is the Holy Father above *Chung Pathien*. It has a parallel meaning and concept with *Yahweh* of the Hebrew people of God like *Pathien Oi* (Pathien Thu Oi) people of God in the messianic people of faith in Christ the anointed one.

[73] Human ministry of the creator God and the nurturing nature of God's care and loving-ministry of life, as life-giving God seen in the person, teachings and work of Christ Jesus are termed as *Humanistry*.

Christ for *gam le nam*[74] is a prophetic ministry of the *Pathien Oi*,[75] messianic people of faith in Christ, the anointed human one. It is a visional prophetic ministry of revealing Christ for the growth and prosperity of the Kukis. It propagates the revelation of people of faith, out of spirituality in Christ for the future well-being of the community people for their self-administrative land. It is a humanistry of people of faith in Christ for *Pathien Oi* people who faithfully trust in the messianic revelation of God in Christ Jesus.

Proclamation of God's love for the well-being of future community in terms of peace, justice and equality is the ministry. It is a humanistry according to the revealing scripture in faith, personal revelation in Christ and future unity in Christ. It is a faithful humanistry in Christ Jesus' nature of truth, which is undying and eternal.

Therefore, KWS can propagate the *houzilja* mission, which is the mission humanistry in Christ for *gam le nam* with special reference to the Kuki messianic people of tribes by tradition and faith. It is because of the Kuki primal theist belief that focuses on the existence of Heavenly/above holy father called

---

[74] Etymologically, the word *Gam* means land, and *nam* refers to people/nation; this term is used by the Kuki people of tribes. *Gam le nam* means Kuki people of tribes who live in the green land of forest. Traditionally, the Kuki people who live in their own land of freedom or independent hill country (*zale'n gam*) live in their way of free life lore dependently; this refers to the Indigenous Kuki Messianic people of *gam le nam* in the love of God in Christ Jesus called *Tahchapa-Jesu* (the true child/son of God).

[75] *Pathien Oi* is spirituality and faith in the messianic child of *Chung Pathien*(God) seen in the person and humanistry of God in Christ Jesus. It is a special term used by the Kuki primal people of the hill village before and during the early times of the spread of Gospel.

Chung Pathien in the *Yahweh* of Hebrew and the Kuki acceptance of the incarnated messianic true child/son of God *Tahchapa-Jesu* in the community of faith called *Pathien Oi* messianic people of God in Christ.

The *Houzilja* mission humanistry in Christ for *gam le nam* is a prophetic ministry that focuses on God and community for the growth and prosperity of the Kuki messianic people of tribes according to the will of God in Christ Jesus. Its ministry is to protect, guide and nurture community life of faith in terms of humanistry for growth and prosperity in the socio-economic, political, scientific and religious life of the people. Its prophetic formative policy is based on the revealing knowledge of God in Christ to uphold love, peace, justice and equality.

All India Kuki Worship Service Coordination Committee Guidelines

Preamble

Having felt the need for all Kuki Worship Services to come together as one in the name of the Lord and Saviour Jesus Christ and in the true spirit of brotherhood or sisterhood, having done the preliminary works towards this end through the initiative of our dedicated leaders (since 2000) and with lots of prayer, we, the Kuki Worship Service located in different cities of India, having given our whole-hearted commitment, join our hearts and minds together under the All India Kuki Worship Service Co-ordination Committee and dedicate ourselves to the following visions:

- To work untiringly for the sipritual and wholisitic development and growth of all the members of our member Units

- To transform each individual member into a blessing for the family, for the Church , for the community in particular and for all others around us

- To worship God with spirit and truth, to serve Him with humility and to glorify Him with majesty, with the help and power of the Holy Spirit

- To harness our resources for strengthening all the KWS Units to be effective agents in the extension of the Kingdom of God.

For the smooth functioning, efficient management and realisation of our visions, goals, aims and objectives of the organisation, which intend to fulfil God's purposes in our lives, and having discussed with and consented to by all the Constituent KWS Units, we hereby, accept to bind ourselves, to adhere to and follow this Constitution in letter and spirit.

Statement of Faith

We believe in:

One God, eternally existent in three persons, Father, Son and Holy Spirit, active in the works of creation, providence and redemption; the Bible as the inspired word of God for teaching, for reproof, for correction and for training in righteousness; the dignity of man and woman created in the image of God, man's subsequent fall and universal sinfulness, his need for justification and regeneration appropriated through personal repentance and faith in Christ, and the resurrection of all people at the return of Christ to eternal life or to eternal condemnation; the spiritual unity of all believers in Christ, composing the Church, the body of Christ, which is visibly expressed in worship, fellowship and service in society.

Article I: The Name

The organisation shall be called All India Kuki Worship Service Co-ordination Committee (hereinafter referred to as the Organisation/Committee)

Article II: Area of Operation and Member Units

The area of operation of the Committee will be all over India. At present, the Committee is constituted by the Kuki Worship

Services located in Shillong, Delhi, Guwahati, Pune, Bangalore, Kolkatta, Happy Valley (Shillong) Hyderabad and so on.

Article III: Aims and Objectives

- To have a common goal for the spiritual development and growth of the members of the KWS Units

- To facilitate the ministry of KWS Units

- To build better relationship and partnership ventures among the KWS's

- To provide all the possible guidance and help to KWS Units

- To organise conferences, seminars, trainings, camps, retreats, etc., and other ancillary services for development of spiritual, social, physical and Godly work as and when possible.

- To have strategic planning and human resources development

- To do acts and things to facilitate the charitable, social, cultural, educational and spiritual services of the Committee, including the management, supervision and administration of its affairs.

- To provide, organise, promote, maintain, manage and render charitable and benevolent services irrespective of race, caste, creed, colour, nationality, community, religion and sex.

- To maintain, administer or establish institutions for the purpose of disseminating Scriptural knowledge and building up believers in their faith.

- To establish practical relationships with organisations having similar aims and objectives

- To undertake relief and rehabilitation measures during natural calamities and disasters, wherever necessary

- To undertake such activities as considered necessary for enhancing the quality of life of all, especially the Kuki people living in different cities of India

Article IV: AIKWSC Committee

- The AIKWSCC Committee will consist of AIKWSCC Executive and AIKWSCC Unit Members

- The AIKWSCC Unit Members will constitute the following: Designated Pastor/Chaplain and Chairman (two Members) of all the KWS Units except those who are already holding any of the above AIKWSCC Executive post. In case where there are no designated pastors/Chaplains, the Secretary shall be considered for the other Unit Membership.

Article V: Functions

Functions of the Committee

- The function of the Committee is to facilitate the ministry of KWS Units

- The Committee will receive the annual ministry reports of KWS Units for information

- The Committee will look into the needs of KWS Units and extend help in whatever way possible.

- The Committee will facilitate the cooperation of all KWS Units; for instance, through organising inter-unit visits, financial support, sharing of prayer, requests, etc.

- The Committee will encourage the Units to achieve their goals

- Apart from their respective functions, it will be the duty and responsibility of all AIKWSCC members to extent cooperation and assist the Committee in discharging its responsibility prudently in every possible ways and means, whenever necessary.

- The function of the Executive Committee is to oversee the administration, management and coordination of different activities and implement guidelines and decisions taken in AIKWSCC.

2. Functions of the Chairman

- The Chairman is the executive head of the organisation and so he will have authority and responsibility for all aspects of the organisation

- He shall conduct all the meetings of the organisation/ Executive Committee

- He is empowered to call general meetings, executive meetings, emergency meetings, etc.

3. Functions of the Vice-Chairman

- The Vice-Chairman will assist the Chairman in every possible way in discharging his duties and responsibilities effectively.

- He can be empowered by the Chairman to function on his behalf in his absence.

4. Functions of the Secretary

- The Secretary shall be responsible for keeping the records of the organisation

- He shall also be responsible for keeping property records

- He shall be responsible for keeping records of minutes of meetings and maintaining registers, statistics, correspondences, files, reports, etc.

5. *Functions of the Assistant Secretary*

- The Assistant Secretary shall assist the Secretary in every possible way in discharging his duties and responsibilities effectively

- He can be empowered by the Secretary top function on his behalf in his absence

6. *Functions of the Finance Secretary-Cum-Treasurer*

i) The Finance Secretary-Cum-Treasurer shall maintain and look after the Cash Book of the organisation.

ii) He shall be responsible for financial receipts and expenditure details and for keeping receipts, cash memo/vouchers/bills, etc., for each transaction

iii) It shall be his or her responsibility to present financial statements/accounts correctly to the Audit Committee.

Article VI: Term of Office

The duration for the AIKWSCC Executive will be three years.

Article VII: Membership

- The membership of the organisation shall consist of those who subscribe to its Statement of Faith and the aims and objectives of the organisation

- Every member of the organisation shall be bound by the provisions of the constitution of the organisation and decisions taken by AIKWSCC from time to time.

- Any individual who is a member of any KWS Unit is automatically a member of the organisation through the Unit to which he or she belongs.

Rights and Privileges of Membership

At any meeting of the organisation, every member present shall have equal vote. The members of the Units shall raise their concern to the meetings through their own respective representatives.

Article VIII: Meetings

The AIKWSCC Meeting will he held once a year. In order to take a decision in the AIKWSCC Executive Meeting or AIKWSCC Meeting, a simple majority of the executive/ Committee should be present.

Article IX: Election System

- Election will be held through nomination by the Election Committee comprising of all the members of AIKWSCC (Executive and Unit Members) to be headed by any one of them, who will be nominated by the outgoing AIKWSCC Executive body.

- Person(s) to be nominated as AIKWSCC Executives should be a member of any one of the KWS Units.

- Person(s) to be nominated as AIKWSCC Executive shall be God-fearing, man of integrity, spiritual and a good Christian

- Any member from the previous AIKWSCC Executive can be re-nominated for the next term in the same capacity or in any other capacity.

- If there is any resignation of the nominated and accepted Executive member, the newly constituted Executive member shall be competent to accept/reject his resignation or take any remedial action deemed appropriate, including nomination of any new person to replace him.

Article X: Audit

The Committee will nominate Audit Committee consisting of three members from the members of the Unit to which the Treasurer belongs. Audit shall be yearly.

Article XI: Funds

The organisation will raise funds by accepting donations, subscriptions, endowments, gifts or voluntary contribution in cash or kind, properties movable and immovable, foundations and bequests from any person, persons, establishments, organisations, institutions or churches for the furtherance of the aims and objectives of the Society and upon such terms and conditions as the organisation in its absolute discretion decides.

Article XII: Obligations

All KWS Units will function independently according to their respective context and needs. However, being a member of this organisation, it is the duty and responsibility of member Units to co-operate and discharge any obligation under this Constitution to enable the organisation to function effectively.

Article XIII: Amendment

The organisation can amend its constitution with the approval of a simple majority of AIKWSCC present in the meeting and the quorum required for effecting Constitution amendment shall be a two-thirds majority of the AIKWSCC. In addition, the proposed amendments shall have to be circulated among all AIKWSCC members in advance.

Article XIV: Dissolutions

In case of dissolution of the organisation, after meeting, all the debts, property and assets of the organisation shall be given to some other organisation(s) with similar objectives or part of them, as decided by AIKWSCC.

Prepared and submitted by
Mr. Lunzalen Khongsai
Rev. J. Lamboi Haokip
October 14, 2005

Future Prospects of Kuki Worship Service

Kuki Worship Service refers to both an individual unit located in a particular place and all the KWS units as a single entity. Let us take a look at the future prospects of KWS.

The Beginning of KWS

KWS-Shillong was started on September 21, 1980. Initially, it was known as Kuki Students Worship Service, Shillong (KSWSS). It was under the aegis of Kuki Students Organisation (KSO), Shillong, that the worship service was formed and functioned.

Though many Kuki students in Shillong at that time attended the English Service conducted by Evangelical Union (EU), Shillong, it was deemed necessary to start a worship service for the Kuki community to facilitate worshipping in one's own language and to provide an avenue for church worship for those students who did not attend the English Service conducted by EU. In order to include family members in the worship service and to facilitate their active participation, the KSWSS was renamed as Kuki Worship Service, Shillong, in 1982. On May 6, 1986, a decision was made to separate KWS from KSO and turn KWS into an autonomous body.

KWS has a non-denominational outlook. Its doors are open to all those who believe in the Father, the Son and the Holy Spirit.

KWS Today

Currently, there are fourteen KWS Units in the cities of Bangalore, Delhi, Guwahati, Happy Valley Shillong, Hyderabad, Kolkata, Mumbai, Pune, Shillong, Itanagar, Silchar and Aizawl. There are two Units outside India—one in London and the other in Kuala Lumpur. As mentioned earlier, the first Unit, the KWS-Shillong, was started in 1980, and the newest Unit, KWS-Pondicherry, was formed in 2011.

Many Units today function as churches, having Sunday Schools for children, prayer cells, women's fellowships, church building projects, missionary activities, social work, etc., besides regular Sunday worship services. Like KWS-Shillong, many of the other Units also have KSO and KWS as two separate autonomous bodies, which work in harmony with each other. In order to foster a better partnership among the various Units, All India Kuki Worship Service Coordination Committee (AIKWSCC) was formed in 2002.

Though AIKWSCC has not been very active, it has facilitated consultations, leadership seminars, closer interactions and exchange of ideas in developing joint projects, common constitution, motto and logo for all the Units. Also, AIKWSCC has been able to interact with different mother churches in Manipur, Nagaland and Assam. It has also coordinated with Kuki Christian Leaders Fellowship (KCLF) to provide chaplains and pastors for various KWS Units and to deal with issues and concerns raised by mother churches.

Future Prospects of KWS

A Non-denominational Worshipping Group with an Inter-denominational Outlook

The word "church" in the English Bible is translated from the term *ekklesia*. This word comes from the Greek word *kaleo* (to call), with the prefix *ek* (out). Thus, the word means "the called out ones." However, the English word "church" does not come from *ekklesia* but from the word *kuriakon*, which means "dedicated to the Lord."

It was also used as a synonym for the word "synagogue", which also means to "come together", i.e., a gathering. It always refers to a local group of believers meeting at a particular geographical location. In the New Testament, the word *ekklesia* is normally used to refer to an assembly of believers. Based on the above definition, KWS is a church, a body of Christians worshipping at a particular location, constituting one congregation.

It provides an alternative for a vibrant community worship that draws around the factors that unite the Kuki community, i.e., faith in Jesus Christ and a common ethnic culture and language. The KWS is located mainly in cities and towns, where the population of the Kuki community is not high. At such places, worshipping as separate groups demarcated along denominational lines will only result in small worshipping groups that may weaken due to lack of numbers.

KWS is thus a non-denominational worshipping group having its members drawn from diverse denominations. As such, KWS should be able to relate with all the denominations of its members and beyond.

Being Called Out and Being Sent Out

KWS consists of a group of people called to worship the Lord Almighty in spirit and truth. "God is Spirit, and his worshipers must worship in spirit and in truth" (John 4:24). KWS is also called to go and make disciples, bringing others into the presence of God to acknowledge and worship Him.

While KWS should concentrate on the Kuki community so that the community's faith is renewed and refreshed, it should also be engaged in mission beyond the Kuki community. This can be done by supporting the ongoing mission of the mother churches or by directly engaging in missionary activities. "Therefore go and make disciples of all nations, baptizing them in the name of the Father and of the Son and of the Holy Spirit ...."(Mathew 28:19).

Focus on Community and Focus on God

KWS plays a unifying role in the Kuki community. It must focus on God, as God is the centre of everything. "Let us fix our eyes on Jesus, the author and perfecter of our faith, who for the joy set before him endured the cross, scorning its shame, and sat down at the right hand of the throne of God" (Hebrews12:2).

Independent and Interdependent

Each Unit of KWS is an independent body, having its own constitution. The individual Units have their own criteria for membership, committees, bylaws, and functions. While preserving this independence, these Units must develop relationships and partnerships among themselves, nurturing mutual understanding and growth.

This presents the possibility of an interdependent movement that seeks to serve God at various KWS locations. The affinity and similar experiences would strengthen the movement, facilitating cross learning. "Each of you should look not only to your own interests, but also to the interests of others" (Philippians 2:4).

Autonomous Identity and Dynamic Relationship

Although KWS and KSO are autonomous bodies, they have a close relationship with each other. This is so mainly because most of the members of KWS are members of KSO as well. This relationship enables KWS to guide, develop and spiritually nurture KSO students.

Exclusive yet Inclusive

Most of the members of KWS come from the Kuki community. In this sense, KWS is exclusive. But this fact should not deter people of other communities or speaking other languages from joining the congregation. There must be an environment of openness, wherein people, including those coming from other communities, feel welcome and accepted.

KWS should also be open to being ministered by non-Kuki groups and denominations. "There is neither Jew nor Greek, slave nor free, male nor female, for you are all one in Christ Jesus" (Galatians 3:28).

Internal Care and External Service

KWS provides brotherly love and care for its members, catering to their spiritual and physical needs. It should also be a platform for serving people outside the Kuki community with the same concern and love. KWS units are located in cities and towns where people from various communities and with different backgrounds reside. It therefore promotes ministry right at the doorstep. "In the same way, let your light shine before men, that they may see your good deeds and praise your Father in heaven" (Mathew 5:16).

Traditional yet Innovative

The functions and worship of KWS imitate traditional practices of home churches, and care should be taken to preserve these traditional values. However, KWS should not be bound by any one traditional method of worship; it must draw from the rich diversities of traditions that the membership represents and should have the freedom to innovate and explore innovative ideas of worship. KWS should incorporate new ideas and practices that can enrich the congregations.

Formal yet Movement-oriented

KWS started as a movement with a tangible pattern of growth, with a sense of direction, aim and progress. It has formulated constitutions and formalised church management structures, pastors, executive committees and various departments; it has also been running diverse projects. Care must be taken not to kill the KWS spirit lest it become too institutionalised.

If it stops progressing, it would stagnate; it would become a still monument, instead of a movement where God is actively at work. God has initiated this movement with a definite purpose. As a body, it should continue to develop and grow unto Christ-likeness. "We will in all things grow up into him who is the Head, that is, Christ" (Ephesians 4:15).

Conclusion

KWS is an avenue for deep spiritual growth. It plays an important role in grooming youth for leading a Christ-like life and for becoming agents of change. It also serves as a model for unity –a model that the churches and the Kuki society can use for forging and strengthening the bonds of friendship. It can also serve as a channel of blessing for society. "I will make you into a great nation and I will bless you; I will make your name great, and you will be a blessing" (Genesis 12:2).

Dino Lunkhosei Touthang

APPENDIX C

Christianity Among Bâwms

The Bâwms worshipped nature for many years, without knowing God. Fortunately, gospel light began to shine on them in 1918 through the work of Wales missionary Edwin Rowlands. According to Darsanglien, the "Thado–Kuki Pioneer Mission" was founded in 1913 by Watkin R. Roberts, who was known as *Sap Tlângval* or the white young man who sailed for India along with Peter Frazer. It is said that after the Mission work gradually expanded in Mizoram and Manipur in 1918, Edwin Rowlands, who was known as *Zo sapthar* or "New Whiteman", was sent by Thado-Kuki Pioneer Mission to visit the Chittagong Hill Tracts, Bangladesh, and give the gospel to the Bâwms.

Since Mission work expanded even outside Manipur — Tripura State and Chittagong Hill Tracts — Roberts changed the name of his Mission, "Thado-Kuki Pioneer Mission", to "North East India General Mission" *(NEIGM)* in 1919.

Regarding the new name of the Mission, Watkin R. Roberts writes:

> As every parents named the name of their children, so I give the name of the field that God gives me. I call it as, North East India General Mission, which sounds pleasant as the parents feel good when they call the name of the child.

It is said that the Mission's name was changed after the Mission expanded to the Chittagong Hill Tracts.

Due to lack of proper written documents, it is very difficult to put the exact date of Edwin Rowlands (Zo Sapthar) and his friend's departure from the Mission headquarters in Manipur for the Chittagong Hill tracts. They probably started at the beginning of December 1918, and after travelling for many days through the thick jungles, they reached the Bâwm village at Vairelh in the Chittagong Hill Tracts on December 12, 1918. In that village, they began preaching the gospel to the Bâwm people, showing Bible pictures and explaining the meanings to them. Later, they also visited some of the neighboring villages, such as Tlângpi, Fiangpidung and Pankhiang. Thus, the gospel entered the Bâwm community in the Chittagong Hill Tracts, Bangladesh. The good news completely changed the spirit of the Bâwm people.

The Establishment of the Bâwm Church

The years 1918-1920 are regarded as a period of silence. So there was lack of continuous ministry among the Bâwms. H. Thangnin, a Bâwm Christian leader, considers this period as a period of "preparation for the gospel of Christ among the Bâwms."

Later in 1921, the North East India General Mission (NEIGM) sent three native missionaries—Pastor Patlaia, Lianthawnga and Saikunga—from Mizoram to the Chittagong Hill Tracts, and the gospel work was resumed among the Bâwm people. Among the Bâwm people, the first converts were Kualthang, Ngunkhar and Tlingbil from Tlângpi village. The new converts were followed by Lalkim, Niangthluai, Saikham, Thawngnin Thangchul, Rotling, Sawmcheu, Ngunfawm and Altlem. These new converts were instruments for spreading the gospel of Christ among their own tribes.

Gradually, the Christian population increased among the Bâwms and on December 24, 1928, the first Christian meeting was held in the form of fellowship and worship of God at Tlângpi village. This was then followed by the first Christmas celebration on the next day, when the twelve new converts were baptised in the name of Jesus Christ. Thus, a new church among the Bâwm people in the Chittagong Hill Tracts came into existence.

As the Bâwm Christian population was increasing day by day, more leaders were needed to look after Mission work. Therefore, in 1929, Pastor. H. Dala who was a student of Dr. Frazer, and Pastor Ruala were sent to the Chittagong Hill Tracts to supervise the Mission work there. After living in the "Mru" area for about ten years, they moved to the Bâwm area in 1939. They lived in Bâwm villages such as Pankhiang, Mualpi, Arthah, Munnuam and Lunginkhar. Ruala replaced Patlaia as the superintendent of the Saichal and Sajek areas, and H. Dala was appointed as the Bâwm area mission field pastoral superintendent. They remained in the same position in the Mission field of the Chittagong Hill Tracts until the white missionary couple, Dr. and Mrs. Pierce D. Samuels, took over charge in 1956.

Dr. and Mrs. Pierce D. Samuels lived at Arthah and Munnuam headquarters in the Chittagong Hill Tracts for about five years. When the Government of Pakistan declared the Hill Tracts to be a restricted area, putting it out of bounds to foreigners, they moved to Chiitagong and lived there until returning to the United States in 1967. In 1965, the Bâwm area Presbytery Committee Meeting adopted the name Evangelical Christian Church (ECC) for the denomination—as stated by Dr. Pierce Samuels in a certificate issued by him on February 2, 1967:

> This is to certify that the Christian works among the Bâwm
> and Pangkhua tribes in the Chittagong Hill Tracts has been

an outgrowth of missionary work under the auspices of the North East India General Mission, which was started in 1918. Subsequently, these efforts, having been blessed by God, have encouraged the Christians to organize their Christian community into Churches following the teaching of the Christian Holy Scriptures. In 1965, they adopted as their Church name Evangelical Christian Church. Since 1962 International Missions Inc. have assisted them and co-operated with them in spiritual advise as well as some other help for teachers, students and some other necessary assistance as Christian brother interested in their spiritual welfare.

Rev. Thimkhup Buiting

APPENDIX D

KWS-Kolkata Decennium 2011 Hymnal

1. *Kum le lha kiheijin, kahin gel doh'uve*
   Muonna lhagao ngaiya, ki bulphu nikho
   Damlai hinkho jemhoijing, van hinna lhagao chun
   Setna a henkolkai, mi hin lhatdoh tan
   Phatna bukim chung Pathien, lei khankho siemhoi
   Neimalsawmna'u houkhawmna, kumsom alhing tai
   (Chung-Pathien) KWS-Kolkata, kum som alhungtai.

2. *Pathien lungsetna chun, eikankhawm jing'uve*
   Eichen khawmpi jing'ui, Khantouna ding'in
   Ngailut, lungset, hepina'n, mitin lungsung hinbawm in
   Lhagao thahatna chun, neisiemhoi jing'un
   Neihin lamkaijun Pakai, Kalalpa'u nahi
   Hinlai khankho siemtup din, kahin saang'uv e
   (Chung-Pathien) KWS-Kolkata, houkhawmna ahi.

3. *Pi le Pu hanna gam, lenkhong gin ngai toh thon*
   Zatam khopi laiya, Pathien-Oi laa in
   Chung Pathien Thu Oi Nammi, hin dounghoi na ding in
   Jesu tahsan lhagao chun, nei hin vai hom un
   Pathien cha Khrista Jesu, Kalalpa'u nang nahi
   Gam le Nam semtup ding in, kahin saang uve
   (Laljesu'n) KWS-Kolkata, hin mapui jing tan.

APPENDIX E

Republic Day Anthem 2011
Bishop's College, Kolkata

(Sung to the tune of *Onward Christian Soldiers*)

1. Blessed land of India prospers in its love
    Land of diversity, republic in Land
    Religion and Culture, traditional life
    Love in diversity is our prosperity

    Onward Bishop's College
    Training for Mission
    In the Spirit of Christ for humanistry

2. From the Southern Coastal plain, hills and vales
    To the Himalayan ranges of the North
    And from Thar Desert and along the Great Plains
    To the North Eastern States, call them all to serve

3. People of God in faith, unite in spirit
    Proclaiming the truth that shows the way and life
    Liberating people for justice and peace
    God in Christ our banner, to serve our country[1]

Ngamkhothang Haokip

---

[1] Amenla Aier,*"Chronicle, 2010-2011. Bishops' College, Kolkata"*, p.23.

A Brief Historical Account of the Kuki Diaspora Group in United Kingdom

***Revd Canon David T Haokip D. D**

Abstract

In the New Testament, the Apostle Paul had written epistles to early churches; likewise, I am writing this article [letter] for people, especially the Kuki community. The diverse experiences of hardship caused by wars, famine and other related problems for centuries forced the Jews to wander in exile (disperse/scatter). In fact, the term "diaspora" refers specifically to the scattering of the Jewish community outside Palestine. But the word "diaspora" is now often used in general cases—in all the cases, it carries the sense of displacement; we can call it "people settled far from their ancestral homelands."

In this article [paper], I want to highlight the gradual dispersal of the Kukis. The Kukis who have migrated from their native land can now be termed as the "Kuki diaspora

---

* The writer is Senior Minister, St George's Parish, Church of England, and Hon. Chaplain, KWS- London.

community." I think there is a divine reason behind this voluntary or involuntary dispersal of our people.

Diaspora Kuki Group in London

London is known to be the global financial centre and the "World politics" hub. We are living in the London borough of Newham. The Newham district comprises around 40 per cent Blacks and other minorities, including us. This group (40 per cent) can be designated as the Diaspora group. As I am from Myanmar, I actively participate in Myanmar Community activities. It is believed that there are a little more than 20,000 Myanmar migrants (Diaspora) in UK. In London, besides Kuki Worship Service, there are quite a few similar fellowships, such as Myanmar Christian Fellowship, Karen Christian Fellowship, Kachin Christian Fellowship, Mizo Christian fellowship and Zomi Christian Fellowship. London also has some community groups; for example, "Burmise community UK", of which I am one of the pioneers. I am the acting pastor and a founder member. The other existing groups include Britain Burma Society, Shan, Karen, Kachin and Chin Community. In addition, there are five Myanmar Buddhist monasteries.

Since I arrived in Britian in 1997, I have looked for Kuki people. I have organised several informal gatherings in my capacity. In April 1998, Pu Paojakhup and Pi Neikim Telien, who are known to be one of the earliest settlers in UK, were assigned the role of "Kuki Chieftainship in UK" in a ceremony accompanied by dedication and prayer (This is our culture and tradition back home). Eventually, this effectively forged the actual development of the Kuki community in the United Kingdom.

Pi Neikim and Pu Paojakhup: A Brief Sketch

Pi Neikim was born at Saikul, Manipur. She is the daughter of Pu Longkhobel Karong, an intellectual who published a book in Thadou Kuki. In 1965, Pi Neikim underwent nurse training in Tezpur, Assam. Her selfless dedication and work ethics eventually led her to earn "UK Nurse Work Permit" in 1967. This caused a fundamental shift in her career. She married Pu Paokhup Telien, who has a post-graduate degree, on 18th August 1973 under the recognition of Church of England holy matrimony. In 1977, after years of constant hard work and commitment, they moved into a decent house. Pi Neikim is surely God-fearing and a woman of principle.

Origin of Kut Celebration in UK

The year 1999 brought us some good fortune: my wife Tinnu and I rented a very beautiful house. We threw a house-warming party. On the same day, we had an informal discussion with our guests—the Kukis we knew and a few students—about the practicality of organising "Kut celebration" at my rented house. To my surprise, none of the guests objected to my proposal. As a result, the first Kut celebration was held on the last weekend of September 1999. For the first three years, I organised the celebration single-handedly. The contribution and efforts made by the first "UK Kut" secretary, Pu Seilen Haokip, Ph. D., are simply unforgettable. We soon realised the importance of Kut celebration: It gave us an opportunity to get together to strengthen community relationships and forge better understanding and friendship within Chin-Kuki-Mizo. Gradually, Kut celebration became a house-after-house affair in my area.

Holding the celebration became easier when Pu Paokhup and Pi Neikim Telien, Pu Kamal Khosla and Pi Shally Bongkim and Pu Tony Litt and Pi Nancy Tinkholhing started taking an active interest in organising the celebration. In 2005, God opened doors for us to serve Him at St George's Parish Church, East Ham, London. Fortunately, the parish has a massive community hall, which we could use as our event venue. This turned Kut celebration into a major modern celebration, attracting over 100 people on each occasion. Since then, a few enthusiastic individuals have started taking initiatives at organising different Kuki events (Chin, Mizo and Zomi). In this regard, Mr. Chonminlien's great contribution towards the celebrations must get a mention. Under God's guidance, the year 2008 saw the UK Kut 10th anniversary celebration; a souvenir was released to commemorate the special event.

At present, the "Kut Committee" is chaired by Revd. Alian Sauntak (Vaiphei) and comprises Secretary Chonminlien Gangte, Information Secretary Ben Guite and Treasurer Tinnu Haokip. Now in UK, the Mizo group has Zo Fate Kut and the Zomi (Tidem Chin) group has Khuado Pwai every year. Also, Chin (Zomi/Kuki) National Day is celebrated in London.

Genesis of KWS-London

We have been fortunate enough to live in St. George's Parish Church Vicarage (Pastor Inn) since we moved in East Ham. We have a spacious garden with a nice shed. The idea of forming Kuki Worship Service started sprouting in the year 2006, when Mr. Chonminlien Gangte and Miss Nenghoi Haokip created a mock banner bearing "KWS London Office" at my garden shed. This funny small insignificant childish act surprisingly began to turn the wheel into a small informal worship group, and later, thoughts for forming KWS-London were aired. Things began to materialise one Sunday afternoon (8th July 2007) when a unanimous decision was reached amongst people attending in different denominations. Pi Neikim Telien led the inauguration service and officially declared the day as the first ever KWS-London fellowship.

On the same day, a committee was formed. Revd. Dr. David T. Haokip was nominated Chairman and Hon. Chaplain. The other portfolios were for Mr Chonminlien Gangte (Secretary),

Miss Neihlam Vaiphei (Treasurer), Mr. Daniel Haokip and Miss Nenghoi Haokip (Worship Leader) and Mrs. Tinnu Haokip (Catering Manager).

KWS Projects

Ever since we began our journey, we witnessed God's blessings in amazing ways—projects that we could manage within our budget. These projects are as follows: The education of Mr. Thangboi Haokip, who is currently serving in Kolkata as KWS Chaplain (BD programme at Kolkata Bishop's college). Mention may be made that a discussion with Revd. Dino L Touthang in London and his recommendation has materialised into sponsoring Mr. Thangboi. It is an undeniable fact that all the efforts made were worthwhile! Indeed, it has resulted in igniting good communication and promoting a sense of oneness across KWS units in India and abroad. Some fund has been released by KWS-London to support charity organisations such as Tabita Children's Home, Imphal and Drug Rehabilitation Shelter, Imphal.

Above all, in various capacities, KWS-London has been involved in financially supporting the formation of KWS, Yangon, Myanmar. Furthermore, we are working hard and looking forward to the formation of the KWS Dhaka and Singapore units as well, for which we would appreciate prayer support.

London-KWS Portfolio 2011-14

The current portfolio holders are as follows: Revd. Canon David T Haokip, Chaplain; Revd. Phillip Zamhao Haokip, Chairman; Chonminlien Gangte, Secretary; Neihlam Vaiphei Garbeldi, Treasurer; Kailean Khongsai, Adviser; Johnny Haolai, Information Secretary; and Daniel Haokip, Music Secretary.

We have above around 20 active members. We gather for fellowship once a month (every second Sunday of the month).

This year, KWS-London celebrated its fourth anniversary on July 9th at Bournemouth Beach.

Global Connection

We are pleased to announce that KWS-London has its own website (www.kwslondon.com). In addition to this, we have kwsnet-egroup. All are welcome! If you want to become a member of this e-group, visit kwsnet subscribe@yahoogroups.com. We use this website for communication and for our ministry.

We are trying hard to build the KWS Global Network. May all the people reading this be blessed. Amen

Thank you all!

Conflict Resolution in North East India

Satkhokai Chongloi

Introduction

The present so-called North East India comprising officially eight states–Arunachal Pradesh, Assam, Meghalaya, Manipur, Mizoram, Nagaland, Sikkim and Tripura–has become a killing field since India's independence in 1947.[1] This region has suffered ever since the withdrawal of the British. It has been known as a 'trouble-torn area', an 'insurgency area', a 'war zone', a 'boiling pot' and so on. Unfortunately, many have not really cared to find out why this region has been regarded as a boiling pot.

The Kuki people, who live not only in North East India, but also in the Chittagong Hill Tracts of Bangladesh and Upper Myanmar, have been victimised by various ruling powers; they have been deprived of their rights.

---

[1] Sikkim became a full state of Indian Union in 1975. It became a member of the regional North Eastern Council in 2003, although not contiguous with the other states of North East India.

The Kuki People and their Country

This region always belonged to the Kuki people. In the Pooyas and Royal Chronicles of the Meitei Kings, Kuki chiefs Kuki Ahongba and Kuki Achouba were allies of Nongba Lairen Pakhangba, the first historically recorded king of the Meitei, in his mobilisation for the throne in 33 A.D. Cheitharol Kumaba (Royal Chronicles of the Meitei Kings) recorded that in the year 186 A.D., Meidungu Taothingmang, a Kuki, became king.[2] Noted historians such as R. C. Majumdar and Blasttasali in "History of India" refer to the Kukis as the earliest people known to have lived in prehistoric India, preceding the Dravidians, whose descendants now live in south India.

Lieut. Col. A. S. Reid says, "Previous to the expedition of 1871-72, the wild tribes, which had been in the habit of raiding our North Eastern Frontier, were generally spoken of as 'Kukis,' a Bengali word, meaning hill men or highlanders."[3] Deputy Commissioner of the Hill Tracts, Captain T. H. Lewin, in 1870, described the Loosei, commonly known as the Kookies, as a powerful and independent people, who touch the borders of the Chittagong Hill Tracts. He added that they (Kookies) extend in numberless hordes into the North and the North-East, until they reach Cachar, on the one hand, and the frontiers of Burma, on the other... they are known to the Bengalees by the name of Kookie and the Burmese as the Lankhe.[4]

---

[2] P. S. Haokip, *Zale'n-Gam the Kuki Nation* (Zale'n-Gam: KNO Publication 2008), 132

[3] A. S. Reid, *Chin-Lushai Land: Including the description of various expeditions in the Chin-Lushai Hills* (India: Calcutta, 1893), 5. Reid also says that the Chin, Lushai were included in the name Kuki since the days of Warren Hanstings and their attack against the British and their subjects dated as far as 1777.

[4] Cited Lewin in T. S. Gangte, *The Kukis of Manipur* (New Delhi: Gyan Publishing House 1993), 20.

In his book, *The Linguistic Survey of India* (Vol. 3, Part 3; 1904), which provides a general idea of the wingspan of the Kuki Country and the composition of its people, G. A. Grierson writes:

The territory inhabited by the Kuki-Chin tribes extends from Naga Hills in the North down into the Sandoway District of Burma in the South, from the Myattha River in the East, almost to the Bay of Bengal in the West. It is almost entirely filled up by hills and mountain ridges, separated by deep valleys. A great chain of mountains suddenly rises from the plains of Eastern Bengal, about 220 miles north of Calcutta, and stretches eastward in a bordering mass of spurs and ridges, called successively the Garo, Khasia and Naga Hills. The elevation of the highest points increases toward the east from about 3,000 feet in the Garo Hills to 8,000 and 9,000 in the region of Manipur. These chain mergers, in the east, into spurs, which the Himalays shoot out from the north of Assam towards the south. From here, a great mass of mountain ridges starts southwards, enclosing the alluvial valley of Manipur, and hence spreads out westward to the south of Sylhet. It then runs due north and south, with cross ridges of smaller elevation through the districts known as the Chin Hills, the Lushai Hills, Hill Tepperah, and the Chittagong Hill Tracts. Farther south the mountainous region continues, through the Arakan Hill tracks, and the Arakan Yoma, until it finally sinks into the sea at cape Negrais , the total of the range being some 700 miles.

The greatest elevation is found to the north of Manipur. Thence, it gradually diminishes towards the south. Where the ridge enters the north of Arakan it again rises with summits upwards of 8,000 feet high, and here a mass of spurs is thrown off in all directions. Towards the south, the western off-shoots diminish in length, leaving a track of alluvial land between them and the sea, while in the north the eastern off-shoots of the Arakan Yoma run down to the banks of Irrawady. This vast mountainous region, from the Jaintia and Naga Hills in the north, is the home of the Kuki-Chin tribes. We find them, besides, in the valley of Manipur , and, in small settlements, in the Cachar plains and Sylhet... Kuki is an Assamese or Bengali term, applied to various hill tribes, such as the Lushais, Rangkhols, Thadous, etc. It seemed to have been known at a comparatively early period. In Ray Mala, Siva is stated to have fallen in love with a Kuki woman, and the Kukis are mentioned in connection with the Tipperah Raja Chachag, who flourished about 1512 A.D.

The Kukis Defending the Independent Hill Country

For centuries, the Kukis had been living in perfect harmony with nature, unaware of the politics of dominance. The Kuki country exists between India and Burma. In the past, writers described it as "Independent Hill Country" or "Kuki Country." The British colonised India and Burma, but a large chunk of the hill country mentioned here was not colonised. Jawaharlal Nehru said, "The Tribal Areas are defined as being those long frontiers of India which are neither part of India nor Burma, or under any foreign power."[5] This was the country the Kukis once protected not only for the Kukis, but also for all the people living in the region. According to historical records, the Kukis defended this country against the British in the early eighteen century. The last and greatest battle was fought during 1917-1919, which the historians call "The Kuki Rising," "The Kuki Rebellions of 1917-1919", or "The Kuki War of Independence."

The Kuki Government vs. the British Government

The first encounter between the Kukis and the British took place during the time when Warren Hastings was the Governor General of British India — the Raja of Chittagong sought British protection against Kuki raids in 1777. Major Kuki raids occurred during 1845-1951.

---

[5] Prasenjit Biswas and C. Joshua Thomas editors, Peace in India's North-East (Regency Publication, New Delhi 2006) 136.

- **The Great Kuki Invasion:** The year 1860 is known as "The Great Kuki Invasion." In this invasion, "15 villages were burnt and plundered, 185 British subjects killed and about 100 captives carried off."[6]

- **Expeditions:** Considering the Kukis as a thorn in the flesh and the difficulties involved in their invasion of the Kuki-Gam, the British started sending military expeditions against the Kukis from 1844. The first major expedition against the Kukis was that of Captain Blackwood's in 1844. Three years later, an expedition was sent under Col. Lister. The other great expeditions were sent in 1860, under Major Raban; in 1868, under General Nutshall; and then in 1871-72.[7]

- **British New Policy:** Expeditions did not bring in amicable peace: More raids reported. In 1871, within a period of thirty days, from January 23 to February 23, the Kukis conducted nine raids and attacked British tea planters, who had intruded into their territorial hunting ground. The British adopted a new divide-and-rule policy in 1889, which eventually divided the Kukiland into three districts: (1) The North Lushai Hills (May 1890), (2) the South Lushai Hills (April 1891) and (3) the Chin Hills (1892-1893).

The Kuki Government in World War I

The Great War with the British broke out in 1917 and lasted till 1919. The war with the Kuki Inpi was the longest war ever fought by the British colonialists in India. In magnitude, it is

---

[6] Lian H. Sakhong, Religion and Politics among the Chin People in Burma- 1896-1949 (Sweden: X-O Graf Tryckeri AB, 2000), 164-165

[7] Karunamay Sinha, *The Sentinel Melange, Magazine vol. xxvii No 9,* (Omega Printer and Publisher, July 26, 2009), 6.

second only to the Sepoy Mutiny.[8] The Kukis' jhumming-based economy could not sustain them any longer; the Kuki Inpi thus stopped the fight. Then the British tried to persuade the Kuki chiefs into adopting a policy of servility by offering them general amnesty, but the Kuki chiefs chose to remain in prison, where many of them died. Some were released after their term of imprisonment was over. So, the Kuki chiefs saved the "Independent Hill Country" through war and imprisonment.

The Kuki Government in World War II

When World War II broke out, the Kukis did not hesitate to fight along with the Indian National Army. The history of Kukis and this country would have been totally different today had the wars been won by the German forces and Netaji Subhas Chandra Bose.

Kukis Traditional Conflict Resolution

The Institution of Salam Sat

The Kuki people regard an adulterer or fornicator as a person of low character, and she or he becomes the object of public ridicule. A Kuki boy who commits adultery with a young unmarried girl is asked to take her as his wife, but if he refuses to marry her, he would need to perform *Salam Sat*, a customary law on adultery, and pay the girl one *Mithun*. If the boy wants to take the girl as his wife and she does not agree, the boy still has to fulfill the strictures of customary law. If the girl is pregnant, she bears and delivers the child and takes care of the child for about three years. Then the boy pays a *Mithun* and a steel gong and takes his child.

If a wife commits adultery willingly, she would be divorced and sent back to her parents without any penalty of divorce.

---

[8] Karunamay Sinha, August 30, 2009, 5.

If she feels sorry, repents of her sins and asks for forgiveness and if her husband forgives her, she can still be his wife. But if she is a rape victim, then the one who raped her has to kill a pig in the Chief's house. His Upa (older brother or head of his family) is fined a Mithun. The Upa of the woman's husband receives the Mithun. This is done because a couple should not play games.

The Institution of Hemkhaam

When one intentionally or unintentionally kills someone, the murderer prevents the victim's family from taking vengeance on the murderer by killing a pig in the chief's house. This act is known as *Hemkhaam* (like today's ceasefire). This *Hemkhaam* has to be done immediately to avoid use of weapons in retaliation. After *Hemkhaam* has been carried out, both parties are bound automatically by the Law of *Hemkham* and the matter is arbitrated in a peaceful manner. The murderer has to give the following for the performance of *Hemkhaam*:

- *Selpi khat* (one *Mithun*) for Kosana

- *Khipi chang ni* (two pieces of bead) for the eyes

- *Dahpi khat* (one gong) for his pillow

- *Pondum khat* (one traditional shawl) for winding sheet[9]

The Institution of Toltheh

The Kukis expend all effort to avoid murder. There is no capital punishment (killing) in the Laws of the Kukis, but life-long *bultuh* (chained to a big log). A person who loses temper and

---

[9] Satkhokai Chongloi, Unpublished Dissertation of D. Min entitled *Culture and Traditional Unity: Context of the Church's Mission Among the Kuki People in Manipur India*, (UTS Philippines, 2003), 38-40

tries to kill or threaten another person is penalised. He has to kill a pig in the Court of the Chief of the village and promise not to continue such behaviour.

If a person is injured and sheds blood while fighting, both parties involved should first make settlement on the shedding of blood before the Village Court judges right or wrong. Because blood spilling defiles the ground, the one who sheds blood has to kill a pig for the institution called "Toltheh." The meaning behind Toltheh is that when blood is shed, the village ground is defiled. When nature is defiled, God is not happy and so nature needs to be cleaned. It is clearly indicated in the incantation of the Toltheh ritual:

> ..na Vohpi maikem bohni solang, alu khonah a paiyin lang chonset kinotdoh tante; ato khotoa paiyin lang chonset kinot lha tante; Pathen thu ahi.

> (... cut your mother pig that has slanted forehead into two halves. Throw the upper halve towards the north of the village, which will push out sins. Throw the lower halve toward the south of the village, which will push out sins. This is the word of God).

Various animals are killed as penalty for violating the law. After the killing, the ritual is performed. As a result, the person is free once again and the environment, which has been defiled, is cleansed. The following incantation shows how nature is restored:

> Tunin phupi akentai phaipi akentai. Kaleiduppi hungthouvin, kaleithopi hungthouvin (The evil elements have retreated today, let the fecundity of my loamy soil be restored).

The Kuki Village Court is one of the fastest courts of the world. It has no cases pending. The Village Court restores the sinner back to his or her normal life and allows humankind to live peacefully with the nature.

Using Traditional Conflict Resolution: Case Studies

Hemkhaam *with the Meitei Community*

Two Kuki youths, namely Paolenlal Chongloi from Keithelmanbi Military Colony and Paokhosat Kipgen from Bongbal Kholen, who were students of NEHU, Shillong, on their way to celebrate Christmas at Bongbal Kholen were unfortunately lynched by Nongbrang Meitei villagers in Thoubal District, Manipur, on December 22, 2009. The two were mistaken for members of the Kuki Militant Group operating in the area. According to the Meteis version, those two youths belonged to a militant group who attacked the villagers and went away in a TATA 704. Contrary to their claim, people of Bongbal kholen and Keithelmanbi Military colony claimed that the two were students of NEHU, Shillong, who came for Christmas holidays and were on their way to Bongbal Kholen to celebrate Christmas.

Tribal social organisations such as KSO, ANSAM, ATSUM, KUMHUR and KMA block the NH-39 for a day, and some of the Metei leaders from UCM and AMUCO, with the help of the government of Manipur, have visited the spot and the victims' families. The government of Manipur took the initiative, and the conflict was solved by performing *Hemkhaam* on December 31, 2009. The Nongbram Meiteis performed *Hemkhaam* by killing a pig and admitted their crime before the Court of the Bongbal Kholen chief. The matter between the two parties was resolved.

Hemkhaam with the Government of Manipur

On September 1, 2004, Jangkholen Chongloi of Khongsai Veng Imphal was pulled down from his house and shot dead in front of his family by the commandos of Imphal East. The Kuki Movement for Human Rights, Kuki Students Organisation and Khongsai Veng Haosa Inpi and the Government of Manipur, represented by Hon'ble Minister Francis Ngajokpa and Hon'ble Minister Ngamthang Haokip, resolved the problem when *Hemkham* was performed by the Government of Manipur.

In a similar manner, two Kuki boys, namely Paominlien Touthang and Lunlal Haokip were shot dead by the police commandos of Imphal West on 26 July 2006 at Langol Laimanai. KSO, AMSU, KUMHUR and KMA with Shri O. Ibobi, Chief Minister, Manipur, reached an agreement and settled the matter after the government of Manipur performed *Hemkham*, a Kuki traditional institution.

Hemkhaam *for Unknown Perpetrators of Killing*

The latest incident happened on the night of November 17 at National Games Village, Manggoulen, when Haokip was shot dead by unknown miscreants. To settle the tension arising out of the killing, the State Government signed a memorandum of agreement with KSO, Imphal, on November 19, 2010.

According to the agreement, the State Government assured that the culprits would be arrested at the earliest possible and the customary *Hemkhaam* would be imposed in order to avoid unwanted incidents. The agreement was signed by President of KSO, Imphal, Helal Khongsai, and General Secretary Seiboi Haokip on behalf of the student body, while IFC/Sports Minister N Biren Singh, TD Minister D.D. Thaisii, MLA of 46 Saikul A/C Doukhomang Khongsai, HAC Chairman Thangminlen Kipgen and MLA of 41-Chandel A/C Thangkholun Haokip on behalf of the State Government.

Kukis' Relationship with Neighbouring Tribes

Kukis' Relationship with the Tripura King

The relationships of Kukis with the Tipperah kings in those days have been recorded in many books. In his book *The Wild Tribes of India*, Dr. Horatio Bickerstaffe Rowney writes:

"Tipperahs are Kookies who own allegiance to Rajah of Tipperah, paying him an annual *nuzzur*, and *abwabs* on marriage and other occasions." It was the king of Tipperah who married a daughter of a Kuki chief. They maintained a much cordial relationship respecting and helping each other's governance. In his book, *The North East Frontier of India*, Alexander Mackenzie has much more on the relationship of Kukis with the Tipperahs.

The kings of Tripura belong to Halam Kuki. They have an elder brother who is always consulted in all matters related to the duties of Upa or elder. The Kuki chiefs ruled under the command of Tripura kings. It was said that every year-end, the Kuki chiefs went to Tripura king and discussed matters related to governance and law and order of the regions. Since the Kukis were known and feared for their military prowess, the neighbouring tribes hired them or asked their assistance when they were in great trouble. The Kukis extended help to the Chakma chief Ramoo Khan, who rebelled against the East India Company in 1777.

Kukis' Relationship with the Meiteis

The Kukis have been neighbours to the Meiteis in Manipur. The Maharajah ruled powerfully in the valley but the Kukis ruled in the hills. They helped one another in times of war. Some incidences can be mentioned at this juncture, such as:

- *Ava lan* (war), the Chahsad Kuki Ningthou (chief) helped the Meitei Ningthou, who fought against the Burmese king. The Chahsad Ningthou killed the Burmese king and brought the head and presented it as a trophy to the Meitei Ningthou.

- In the war against the Assamese Abhor king, the Kukis again helped the Meitei king. Even when the Chin king abducted Chandrakirty Singh, 1,200 Kuki warriors went to his rescue and brought the Meitei king back to his throne.

Even in post-independent India, the Kukis opposed the Meitei king to sign a merger agreement. The Kuki chiefs led by the Chahsad chief tried their level best to stop the Maharajah Bodha Chandra for signing the merger agreement. At last, the king went to Shillong and signed the merger agreement on September 21, 1949. Eventually, Manipur valley was merged fully with Indian Union on October 15, 1949, but the Hills remained under the rule of the Kuki chiefs.

The present Manipur state is dominated mainly by the Meitei community who are two-third of the whole population of Manipur, occupying the valley, which is hardly 10 per cent land of the state. Since India is a democratic country and where heads are counted, the valley Meiteis in the state Assembly has 40 seats and another 20 seats goes for Outer Manipur, who are tribal Kukis and Nagas. Most of the government offices, educational institutions, hospitals, etc., have been located in Imphal, the capital city of Manipur. Moreover, some of the smaller Kuki towns, such as Moreh, Churachandpur, Kangpokpi, Saikul and Motbung, are proposed to be declared as urban towns.

The militant groups of the valley also planted landmines in the Kuki area in Chandel District. More than 30 Kuki civilians were killed and many more people handicapped for life. The militants also gang-raped about 20 Kuki girls in the Palbung area and a young mother in the Churachandpur district of Manipur. The Kukis have apprehension about the new development, which they believe will not work for peaceful coexistence. The Kukis endured hardship with maximum patience for peaceful coexistence.

Kukis' Relationship with the Nagas

Kukis have maintained a cordial relationship with the Nagas. The cordial relationship of the Kukis with the Mao and Paumai Naga people is evident in the inscription on the 16-foot-high stone at Pudunamai village, where names of chiefs who signed the Peace Treaty with them were inscribed. There is also a list of Kuki chiefs. It is a living monument of peace and tranquility upheld between the Kukis and the Mao and Paumai Nagas.

Kukis' Relationships With Semomas and other Naga Tribes

Secondly, the Kukis have a good relationship with the Semomas. They signed an alliance agreement of brotherhood; Pu (L) Mangkhokai from the Kukis side and Pu (L) Dopulie Hepie from the Semomas side were the signatories. The others could be seen between the Jampi chief and the Tening chiefs of the present Nagaland. The Tening people received inhuman treatment from their fellow Nagas. It was said that these weaker Naga villages were vulnerable to rape, loot and attack from the stronger Naga tribes. They make peace with the Jampi chief and the Jampi chief protected Tening village. Therefore, the Tening chief, in appreciation and gratitude, offered a piece of land to the Jampi chief, which is a living symbol of the love and peace between them.

The Kuki chief of Jampi Pu (L) Thusong Sitlhou reached a peace treaty with the Khonoma village to help and protect one another's village from invaders. The Khonoma chief and the Jampi chief drank water together from a gun's barrel as oath–as a symbol of peace treaty.

The Kukis have a religious relationship with the Zeliang. They formed Kuki-Zeliang Association during 1936-1953. While the Kukis were engaged in war against the British, the Naga leaders formed the Naga Club in 1918. The historic memorandum to the Simon Commission, which I believe was the basis for all subsequent political struggles of the Nagas, was submitted in 1929, where a Kuki leader, Pu Lengjang Khongsai Kuki, was one of the signatories. The Kukis in Nagaland have been a part of the Nagas' political struggles since then. The cordial relationship could be seen in many incidents. For instance, the Kukis joined together with Semas and Rengmas (Sekureng) for administrative convenience.

Present Relationship with the Nagas

The century-old peace between the tribals living in Manipur hills was disrupted when the United Naga Council, Manipur, served a "Quit Notice" to the Kukis on October 22, 1992. Eventually, the NSCN (I-M) has started killing the Kukis. More than 900 Kukis have been killed and more than 360 villages have been uprooted so far.

The Kuki Inpi was revived on June 29, 1993, with its traditional government policy:

- Kuki Inpi is non-communal

- Peaceful coexistence

- Justice for all

The Kuki Inpi Manipur (KIM) took the initiative to have consultation with the UNC-M. The first consultation meeting was held at Manipur Baptist Council Conference Hall on March 29, 1994. The second meeting was held at Kuki Christian Church Assembly Hall on April 4, 1994, where UNC-M informed the Kuki Inpi that they were not allowed to attend this meeting by the NSCN (I-M) and that they could not continue meeting with the Kuki Inpi Manipur.

The then Kuki Inpi President Pu T. Kipgen advised UNC-M to contact KIM as and when UNC-M was permitted and ready to have consultation on the issue why UNC-M was compelled to wage war against the Kukis. After one of the

Committee for Restoration of Normalcy (CRN) meetings at MBC Centre, the Vice President of Kuki Inpi Pu Lalkhohen Thangeo was kidnapped and on the following day, his body was found in one of the ponds near Muslim Cemetery in Imphal.

In response to the daily news of the 'Kuki-Naga conflict,' the Kuki Inpi, Manipur, declared that there was no conflict between the Kukis and the Nagas. They believed that the term 'conflict' has been coined by some social elements just to paint the movement of the Nagas' self-determination as conflict with the Kukis. Many from the Kuki and Naga communities were killed because of the movement of NSCN (I-M).

One very serious violation of human rights that all civilised citizens in the 21st century should strongly condemn is what had happened to the people of Kanjang and neighboring Kuki villages. The Kukis of this area had been forced to be converted into Puchery Naga tribe. They were forced to use the Puchery Bible and sing Puchery songs in their Church services. It has to be condemned strongly, and the Nagas should stop doing it and recognise the Kukis as Kukis only.

UNC-M and KIM have recently started meeting together to discuss issues such as what has compelled the United Naga Council, Manipur, to wage war against the Kukis, their future and how to restore peace and harmony in their land.

Causes and Concerns of Conflict in North East India

World Wars I and II brought about changes in some parts of the world. The creation of India and Burma was one of them, which annexed a part of the Independent Hill country into Indian Union; part of which into the then Burma and part of which into Bangladesh without the consent of the indigenous people of the region. Some of the causes of conflicts lie in the separation and creation of states and boundaries. The region has witnessed a lot of violence, and some of the causes of this violence are mentioned below:

The First Main Cause of Conflict: The Land Issue

- North East India is connected to the Indian mainland by a narrow corridor called "Chickens' neck." The region shared 90 per cent of its boundaries with the surrounding foreign countries. North East India is also influenced by (a) the pragmatic and realistic communism of China in the north, (b) the calm and spiritual Buddhism of Myanmar in the East, (c) the religious and irreconcilable Islam of Bangladesh in the South and (d) the rational and philosophical Hinduism of the Hindus in the West. No wonder we have endless conflicts in the region. Under these circumstances, the Christians of the region have miles to go; they must stand together.

- Most people of North East India are classified as Scheduled Tribes by the Indian law of classification. However, they are not tribal as such. They are landlords. The land does not belong to them; they belong to the land. Militant groups operate in the region because of the land issue. They fear that their land would be controlled by someone else. Conflicts happen when outsiders frame policies to divide the region and rule over it. It is to protect their ancestral lands that militant groups operate in the region today.

- All militant groups in the region face one common issue— "defending the land." They have been protecting this region for centuries and want to live in peace. The land issue can be addressed if all militant groups have dialogues with one another and find common denominators whereby they can collectively defend their land.

The Second Main Cause of Conflict: Marginalisation

- The Bengal Eastern Frontier Regulation Act 1873 was passed to protect the tribal lands of North East India. The Act, which was introduced as "Inner line Permit" in lieu of the passport of the present day to bar outsiders (non-residents) from entering the region, has been changed into "Protected Area Permit", which means the people living in the region are under someone's protection.

- Taken gradually, the whole region fell into Indian Union, Myanmar or Bangladesh. Manipur and Tripura merged into Indian Union on October 15, 1949. Mizoram on February 20, 1987. Bangladesh was born on March 26, 1971, and the Kukis of Chittagong Hill Tracts were included without their knowledge and consent.

Peace Accord Used For Conflict Resolution: A Failure in North East India

Many peace accords have been signed in North East India since 1947, but they all have witnessed nothing but failure.

- Naga Peace Accords: The three accords signed by the Naga rebel groups (in 1947, 1960 and 1975) did not bring amicable solution to the problems faced by the Nagas.[10] Nagaland became a full state of the Indian Union on December 1, 1963.

---

[10] In 1947, the Naga National Council, comprising eleven tribes, signed a nine-point agreement, which was also known as Naga-Akbar Hydari Accord, with the Governor of Assam, Akbar Hydari. The ten-year period of agreement was interpreted in different ways. The Nagas thought that they will have independence after ten years, when the agreement ends. The Indian side was ready to give the Sixth Scheduled type of administration to the Nagas. The sixteen-point agreement was signed between the Government of India and the Naga People's Convention in 1960, which the Naga National Council refused to recognise. The next accord was "The Shillong Accord", which was signed in 1975.

- The Mizo Peace Accord: The Mizo Peace Accord was signed between Mizo National Front led by Pu Laldenga and Government of India in 1986, which marked the end of the 20-year-long insurrection in the entire state of Mizoram. Mizoram became a full state of the Indian Union on February 20, 1987, but sections of MNF are still against the accord.

- The mass surrender of Bodo Liberation Tigers on December 3, 2003, created Bodo Territorial Council; some rebels were against this creation.

States in North East India Named After Community or Tribe: A Failure

Have peace accords really contributed towards bringing peace to the region or have they created more misunderstanding and tension? The present scenario of North East India answers the above question.

- Government of India signed peace accords with tribes who have been dissatisfied with present governance and harbour militants. The Government of India tends to seek solution to the last sighted provocation rather than addressing the root cause of conflict in the region, which creates enmity between tribes living together peacefully from time immemorial.

- Peace accords have never been signed with the loyal citizens living in the region. All accords have been signed with rebel groups. This prompts loyal citizens to take a violent path to draw the attention of the Government towards the issues faced by them –to eventually have a dialogue with them.

- After the signing of peace accords, statehood or the like was given to the rebel groups and the state was named after their tribe, such as Nagaland for the Nagas and Mizoram for the Mizos. Were there people other than the

Mizos living in Mizoram and were there tribes other than the Nagas living in Nagaland? Did they witness peace after the signing of those accords? Then why are the Hmar People's Council and the Brus not happy in Mizoram? Can Government of India sign peace accords with all the tribes (more than 400 indigenous tribes) in the region just to make them happy?

Conclusion

The issues related to North East India cannot be resolved on a piecemeal basis. It has to be done collectively. These issues stem from the lives and cultures of people groups living together from time immemorial. They cannot be resolved by outsiders. New Delhi, Yangon and Dhaka cannot offer a lasting political solution, as they do not understand the people of this region well; only the indigenous people know what it means to live in this region. So they are the ones who should offer a solution.

A non-territorial style of governance, where all people groups take part in decision-making, should be adopted. Unless our movement is for the people, by the people and of the people living in this region, the issues we face today will never be resolved. The Kukis have been closely monitoring all local movements, but they need to review their stand on the issues we face today, especially conflict resolution.

The writer is Senior Lecturer of ministries, Trulock Theological Seminary, Imphal; Secretary, Social Concern of Kuki Christian Leaders' Fellowship; General Secretary, Kuki Movement for Human Rights; and Chairman, Kuki Nampi Palai.

Note: This paper was presented at a seminar on "Peace Making in North East India" held at Eastern Theological Seminary, Jorhat, Assam, during December 1-4, 2010.

APPENDIX H

Area of Operation, British India

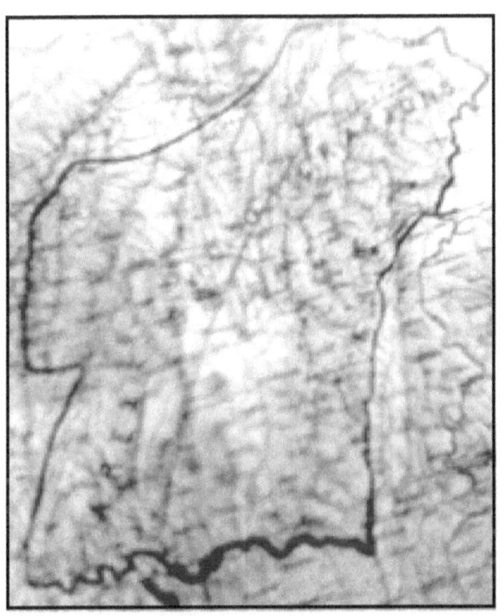

**Map Showing Kukis' Area of Operation by
the British Raj**

Abstract from

Jangkholam Haokip, *A Theological Study of Identity among the Tribal People of NorthEast India with a Special Reference to The Kukis of Manipur.* Ph. D Thesis, University of Aberdeen, Scotland 2010.

Bibliography

BOOKS

Chongloi, Hemkhochon *Indoi. A study of primal Kuki religious symbolism in the hermeneutical framework of Mircea Eliade*. Delhi: ISPCK, 2008.

Clintock, Mc and Strong Encyclopedia, *Electronic Database*. Bible soft Inc. 2000 to 2006.

Dun, E.W. *Gazetteer of Manipur*, Delhi: Vivek Publication Company, 1981.

Erdman, Wm. B.*International Standard Bible Encyclopaedia*. Publishing Co. 1979.

Elly, E.B. *Military Report on the Chin-Lushai Country*, Calcutta: KLM Pvt. Ltd, 1978.

Gangte, T.S. *The Kukis in Manipur, a historical analysis*. Gyan Publishing House, 1993.

Grierson, G.A. *Linguistic Survey of India*, Vol. III. Calcutta: Asiatic Society, Part-3.

Goswami, Tarun. *Kuki Life and Lore*. Haflong: NC Hills District Council, Assam 1985.

Haokip, Seilen. *Rhetoric of Kuki Nationalism, A treatise*. New Delhi: Lustra Print, 2010.

Haokip, P.S. *Zale'n Gam The Kuki Nation*, Zale'n Gam: KNO Publication, 2008.

Haokip, Paolen. *Karl Barth understanding of 'the word of God' and its relevance for Kuki understanding of Pathen thu (word of God) today*. Unpublished Thesis: Senate of Serampore, NIIPGTS, Serampur, 2009

Haolai, Henkhovum, *Assam Gam a Kukite Thusim*. Halflong: Mungrati Press, 2009.

Halley, Henry H. *Halley's Bible Handbook*. Michigan: OM Books India, 1999.

Majundar, RC & N Bhattacharya, *History of India*. N.p: 1930.

Mate, Lhunkhosei *A study on Sabasten Kappen's understanding of Culture and its relevance for Kuki Culture in Manipur"* (M.Th Thesis of Senate of Serampore College, 2011)

Rowney, Horatio Bickerstaffe. *The Wild Tribes of India*. Delhi: Low Price Publication,1982.

Shaw, William. *Notes on the Thadou-Kukis*. Guwahati: Maranatha Printing Press, 1929.

KUMHUR, The plight of *The Indigenous Kuki People, unraveling the story of deception, suppression and marginalization in the trio Border Areas of India, Myanmar and Bangladesh*. Imphal: Kuki Movements for Human Rights, 2009.

_______________, *The Kuki People and their country*. Washington DC: The Publicity wing Kuki Movement for human rights, 2005.

Vaiphei, Kim. *The coming of Christianity in Manipur; with special reference to the Kukis*. New Delhi: The Join Women's Programme, 1995.

Souvenir

Aier, Amenla *Chronicle, 2010-2011 Bishops' College Kolkata*

_______________, Decade Souvenir, 1999-2009. Hyderabad: KWS Hyderabad, 2009.

_______________, Khanglai 2008 cum KWS-G Decade Celebration Souvenir, 2008. Guwahati: KWS Guwahati 2008.

_______________, Ahsijolneng, Annual Magazine 2007. Shillong: A Publication of Kuki Students' Organization, 2007.

_______________, Decade Celebration Souvenir, 1999-2009. Bangalore: KWS Bangalore, 2009.

_______________, Church Inauguration Souvenir, Guwahati: KWS-G 2010.

_______________, Reports of Seminar on Manmasi Identity. Imphal: LB Printer, 2009.

___________, Ebenezer, Decade Celebration Souvenir 1992-9002. Delhi: KWSD 9002.

Letters and Mail

Gangte, Chonminlen "KWS-London" (July 28, 2010).

Haokip, Tongmang. "Pathen Oi Ngailutna Chibai" (May 12, 2010). Personal mail to the author (June 16, 2010).

H.S.Yampao. "Thatepna" (January 20, 2009) Personal mail to the author (January 30, 2009).

Haokip, Lalboi "Formation of KWS Chennai" (August 14, 2010) Personal mail to the author. (August 20, 2010).

Haokip, Letlal. "KWS Delhi Activities" (August 03, 2010) Personal mail to the author, (04 August 2010).

H. Yampao "KWS Yangon Thusim" (July 26, 2011).

Lhungdim, Mangboi, 'KWS Chennai Akipatdan' (August 10, 2010) Personal mail to the Author (August 13, 2010).

Lunkim, T. "Kukite Sahnit Nikho" (September 8, 2009) Personal letter to the author. (September 10, 2009).

Lhungdim, T. "Brief history of KWS Mumbai" (July 27, 2010) Personal mail to the author. (July 30, 2010).

Lun Neh "KWS-Yangon Chung Chang Thu" (August 3, 2011).

Personal Interview

B. Lalnunzira, Lecturer O.T. Bishop's College, Kolkata. Interview, July 11, 2010.

Chongloi, Hemkhochon. Teacher & Librarian TTS at KCC Imphal. Interview, July 5, 2010.

Chungthang Thiek, Secy. EFI NEI Guwahati, Interview, July 15, 2010.

Haokip P. Tongmang, Vice Rector OTC Mawlai. Interview, May 11, 2010.

Hawlngam Haokip, Leader of KBC Manipur. Interview, June 10, 2009.

Jamneng (90) Wife of (L) Holngam Haokip a local Church founder of Maokot Ukhrul Dist. Manipur at Tuinom Lamka, Interview. May 24, 2010.

Kipgen Thangsat. General Secy. KBC Manipur. Interview. June 16, 2010.

Lunkim, T. Chairman KUMHUR and Adm. Secy. KCC Imphal. Interview. May 30, 2010.

Samte, Lian. Assistant Secy. Zomi Fellowship Kolkata. Interview October 03, 2010.

Singsit, Lunkhoseh. Church Leader of Motbung. Interview, July 06, 2010.

Singson, Seikholet. KBC Founder at Buongmol, Interview, June 01, 2010.

Vaiphei, Prime. President AMCO Imphal. Interview, June 06, 2010.

Vaiphei, Biaka Field Secy. UPC Kolkata. Interview, September 19, 2010.

Telephonic Interview

Chongloi, Kamchon Chairman KWS-Silchar. Telephonic Interview, August 21, 2010, 8:30-9:00 AM.

Gangte, Lalboi. Join Secy. AIKWSCC. Telephonic Interview, August 21, 2010 9:30 AM.

Guite, Jamkhosei Pastor KWS Shillong, Telephonic Interview, August 21, 2010.

Haokip, Paothang. Secretary AIKWSCC. Telephonic Interview, August 17, 2010 8:00 AM.

Hangsing, Asat Pastor KWS Itanagar, Telephonic Interview, October 28, 2010. 9-10 AM.

Khongsai, Lunjalen Secretary KWS Guwahati. Telephonic Interview, August 19, 2010. 9:00 PM.

Other Sources

Chongloi Satkhokai, *Conflict Resolution in North East India: Perspective of the Kukis.*

KWS-K Secretary Record: Minutes of the General Meeting. Colinga Baptist Church. August 23, 2006.

The Telegraph January 17, 1994.

Electronic Sources

http://en.wikipedia.org/wiki/Kuki (August 10, 2010. 1535 hr)

http://www.kukination.net/government.php (August 10, 2010. 1530 hr.)

http://www.kukination.net/culture.php (August 10, 2010. 1523 hr.)

http://www.kukiforum.com (November 2, 2010. 1903 hr)
http://www.e-pao.net (September 3, 2010. 2015 hr)
www. kwslondon.com (August 6, 2011. 1530 hr)

www.ingramcontent.com/pod-product-compliance
Lightning Source LLC
Chambersburg PA
CBHW031310160726
47993CB00001B/361